The following is simply a checklist for what to watch out for. You may have to look at more specific .s to find a greater discussion and more detailed analysis.

1. Obama care mandate for 2015.

Those who do not purchase health insurance during 2015 are subject to a tax penalty in 2015. The penalty amount for 2015 is increased to the lesser of 2% of your income or $325 per adult and $162.50 per dependent under age 18 living in your household. However, the penalty is capped at the national average premium, which is $207 per individual (up from $204 per individual in 2014).

2. Itemized medical expenses. For 2015, the rate for medical driving is 23 cents per mile (a half cent less than in 2014).

3. Long-term care coverage. The portion of long-term care insurance premiums that are treated as a deductible medical expense has increased slightly in 2015 for each age group.
4. Flexible spending arrangements (FSAs). In 2015, the maximum salary contribution to an FSA is limited to $2,550 (up from $2,500 in 2014).

5. Health savings accounts and Archer medical savings accounts. The contribution limits for HSAs and MSAs in 2015 have been increased slightly.
6. Accelerated death benefits. For chronically ill individuals, the daily dollar limit excludable from gross income for 2015 is $330. Amounts in excess are taxable to the extent they exceed actual long-term care costs.

7. ABLE (Achieving a Better Life Experience). It is designed to help pay costs of a person who is disabled with blindness or a disability under the Social Security Act, where a person has a disability on file with the IRS (look for further clarification in the coming months). Contributions are not tax deductible, but withdrawals to pay qualified expenses are tax free much like Disability payments. Deductible expenses are the costs for health, education, and welfare.

8. American opportunity credit. There is no modified adjusted gross income limit change in 2015 for eligibility to claim the credit
9. Lifetime learning credit. The modified adjusted gross income limits on eligibility to claim the credit have been increased slightly for 2015.

10. Tuition and fees deduction. The above-the-line deduction for tuition and fees of up to $4,000 for
2015 is not yet extended as of 12/25/2015. Based on the previous year (an also an election year coming up in 2016, the odds are this deduction will remain to get the "younger vote out".

11. Student loan interest. There is no modified adjusted gross income (magi) limit change in 2015 The deduction remains the same and unchanged.
12. Interest on U.S. savings bonds. The MAGI limits on the claim of exclusion for interest on bonds redeemed to pay higher education costs have been increased for 2015.

13. Mortgage insurance. The ability to treat mortgage insurance as deductible mortgage interest has not been determined as yet for 2015. The fallout would generate enough front page news that it is unlikely it will be removed from

the tax deductions for 2015. However, stranger things have happened when one party is trying to blame the other political party for not getting things done. Wait and see, it should be interesting. A loan modification in and of itself does not give rise to an actual interest deduction until that interest is actually paid.

14. Cancellation of mortgage debt. The foreclosure and debt forgiveness or Cancellation of a debt may still be excluded into 2015 if Congress extends the 2014 expiration. The verdict is still out if this law will be extended for 2015 or not. Currently, it appears it will.

15. Moving expenses. Use of a vehicle for deductible moving purposes in 2015 is figured at the rate of 23 cents per mile (a half cent less than in 2014).

16. Energy improvements. The residential energy property credit for adding insulation or installing energy-efficient windows and exterior doors, is up for grabs. The verdict is still out if this law will be extended for 2015 or not. Currently, it appears it will.

17. Parsonage allowance. Members of the clergy can exclude housing allowance they receive.
18. Traditional IRAs and Roth IRAs. MAGI limits on contributions have increased for 2015. There is no change to the contribution limit of $5,500 or to the "catch-up" limit of $1,000 for 50 years old by the end of 2015. It does however limit rollovers to one per taxpayer starting in 2015

19. 401(k) and similar plans. The 2015 elective deferral contribution limit and additional contribution limit for age 50 or older have been increased to $18,000 and $6,000,.
20. Self-employed retirement plans. Contribution, benefit, and other limits for these plans have been increased for 2015.
21. Simplified Employee Pension plans (SEPs). Contribution limits for these plans have been increased for 2015. Earnings threshold for including an employee in a SEP have also been increased.

22. Savings Incentive Match Plans for Employees (SIMPLEs). Contribution limit for SIMPLEs and the additional contribution limit for those age 50 or older by the end of the year 2015 are increased to $12,500 and $3,000 each.

23. Retirement saver's credit. The MAGI limits have been increased for

2015.

24. Charitable transfers of IRA distributions. The rule allowing those age 701/2 and older to transfer up to $100,000 of IRA funds directly to a public charity on a tax-free basis is still up in the air. The verdict is still out if this law will be extended for 2015 or not. Currently, it appears it will.

25. Business use of your personal car. The standard mileage ratein 2015 is 57.5¢ per mile (a penny and a half more than in 2014).
26. Business travel per diem rates. The maximum federal per diem rate for travel is $129 per day ($83 for lodging and $46 for meals).
27. Driving your car for medical or moving purposes. The IRS standard mileage rate for 2015 is 23 cents per mile.
28. Equipment purchases. Two key changes impact write-offs for equipment purchases in 2015:

First-year expensing. The $500,000 limit was extended retroactively for 2014 and unless it is extended again, the limit for the Section 179 deduction in 2015 will be $25,000 and this limit will phase out when purchases exceed $200,000.

29. Bonus depreciation. Bonus depreciation was extended for 2014. The verdict is still out if this law will be extended for 2015 or not. Currently, it appears it will. Bonus depreciation—50% deduction
30. Self-employment tax. The self-employment tax in 2015 is $118,500 (up from $117,000 in 2014).

31. Standard mileage rate. the standard mileage rate, for 2015; it is 57.5¢ cents per mile (a cent and a half more than in 2014). Those who use the standard mileage rate for 2015 must reduce the vehicle's basis by 24¢ per mile (the rate in 2014 was 22¢ per mile).
32. State and local sales taxes. Unless Congress extends the deduction of State and Local Taxes, it will expire on Dec. 31, 2014 and not be usable for your 2015 tax returns. This is a pretty widely known deduction and well used so the likelihood of not being extended seems rather remote.

33. Gifts you receive. The annual exclusion amount for 2015 is $14,000 per recipient (the same as in 2014).
34. Standard deduction amounts. The basic standard deduction amounts for 2015 have been increased for all filing statuses:

- Married filing jointly and surviving spouses: $12,600
- Heads of households: $9,250
- Singles and married filing separately: $6,300

Additional standard deduction amounts. For 2015, the additional standard deduction amount for age and/or blindness remains unchanged at $1,550 for single filers and heads of households, but for married filers (filing jointly or separately) and surviving spouses, it has increased to $1,250.

35. Earned income credit. The earned income credit amounts, including adjusted gross income limits, have been increased for 2015.
36. Educator expenses up to $250—deductible as an adjustment to gross income
37. Energy-efficient buildings—deduction up to $1.80 per square foot
38. First-year expensing—enhanced deduction
39. IRA transfers directly to charity by those age 701/2—tax free up to $100,000

Introduction
To determine if you can take the PTC, see the Can You Take the PTC, later, and Form 8962 and its separate instructions.
This . provides additional information to help you determine if your health care coverage is minimum essential coverage.

This . also provides additional instructions for taxpayers in the following special situations.
- Taxpayers who are filing a separate return from their spouses because of domestic abuse or abandonment.

- Taxpayers who must repay excess APTC and want to determine their eligibility for penalty relief.
- Taxpayers who need to calculate PTC and APTC for a policy that covered an individual not lawfully present in the United States.
- Taxpayers who are filing a tax return but who are not claiming any personal exemptions.
- Taxpayers who need to determine the applicable second lowest cost silver plan (SLCSP) premium.
- Taxpayers who need to allocate policy amounts because one qualified health plan covers individuals from three or more tax families in the same

month.

• Taxpayers who married during the tax year and want to use an alternative calculation that may lower their taxes.

• Self-employed taxpayers.

Table of Contents

Under the health care law, certain health coverage is called minimum essential coverage (MEC). You generally cannot take the PTC for an individual in your tax family for any month that the individual is eligible for minimum essential coverage, except for coverage in the individual market, defined below. Minimum essential coverage means coverage under any of the following programs.

• Health plans offered in the individual market.
• Grandfathered health plans.
• Government-sponsored programs.
• Employer-sponsored plans.
• Other health coverage designated by the Department of Health and Human Services as minimum essential coverage.

Minimum essential coverage does not include coverage consisting solely of excepted benefits. Excepted benefits include stand-alone vision and dental plans (except pediatric dental coverage), workers' compensation coverage, and coverage limited to a specified disease or illness. You may have any of these types of coverage and also get the PTC for your coverage in a qualified health plan.

Note.
Your minimum essential coverage may be reported to you on Form 1095-A or, generally beginning for coverage in 2015, on Form 1095-B or Form 1095-C.

## Individual Market Plans

A health plan offered in the individual market is health insurance coverage provided to an individual by a health insurance issuer licensed by a state, including a qualified health plan offered through the Marketplace. Even though these plans are MEC, eligibility for coverage in the individual market does not prevent an individual from qualifying for the PTC for coverage in a qualified health plan purchased through the Marketplace.

## Grandfathered Health Plan

A grandfathered health plan means any group health plan or group health insurance coverage to which section 1251 of the Affordable Care Act applies (in general, health insurance or self-insured employer coverage that an individual was enrolled in on March 23, 2010).

## Government-Sponsored Programs

Government-sponsored programs are the following. 1. Medicare Part A.
2. Medicaid, except for the following programs.
a. Optional coverage of family planning services.
b. Optional coverage of tuberculosis-related services.
c. Coverage of pregnancy-related services in states that do not provide full Medicaid benefits on the basis of pregnancy.
d. Coverage limited to the treatment of emergency medical conditions.
e. Coverage of medically-needy individuals (except in states where, beginning in 2015, Medicaid for medically-needy individuals is designated as MEC).
f. Coverage under a section 1115 demonstration waiver program.
Call your state Medicaid office if you have any questions.
3. The Children's Health Insurance Program (CHIP).
4. Coverage under the TRICARE program, except for the following programs.
a. Coverage on a space-available basis in a military treatment facility for individuals who are not eligible for TRICARE coverage for private sector care.
b. Coverage for a line of duty related injury, illness, or disease for individuals who have left active duty.
5. The following coverage administered by the Department of Veterans Affairs.

a. Coverage consisting of the medical benefits package for eligible veterans.

b. Civilian Health and Medical Program of the Department of Veterans Affairs (CHAMPVA).

c. Comprehensive health care for children suffering from spina bifida who are the children of Vietnam veterans and veterans of covered service in Korea.

6. A health plan for Peace Corps volunteers.

7. The Nonappropriated Fund Health Benefits Program of the Department of Defense. (This program is both government-sponsored coverage and employer-sponsored coverage.)

In general, you are eligible for a government-sponsored program if you meet the criteria for coverage under one of the programs listed above. If you can be covered under one of these programs you cannot get the PTC for your coverage in a qualified health plan. But see Exceptions , later. However, you will not lose the PTC for your coverage until the first day of the first full month you can receive benefits under the government program. If you can be covered under a government-sponsored program, you must complete the requirements necessary to receive benefits (for example, submitting an application or providing required information) by the last day of the third full calendar month following the event that establishes eligibility (for example, becoming eligible for Medicare when you turn 65). If you do not complete the necessary requirements in this time, you will lose the PTC for your coverage in a qualified health plan beginning with the first day of the fourth calendar month following the event that makes you eligible for the government coverage.

Example 1.

Ellen was enrolled in a qualified health plan with APTC. She turned 65 on June 3 and became eligible for Medicare. Ellen must apply to Medicare to receive benefits. She applied to Medicare in September and was eligible to receive Medicare benefits beginning on December 1. Ellen completed the requirements necessary to receive Medicare benefits by September 30 (the last day of the third full calendar month after the event that established her eligibility, turning 65). She was eligible for Medicare coverage on December 1, the first day of the first full month that she could receive benefits. Thus, Ellen can get the PTC for her coverage in the qualified health plan for January through November. Beginning in December, Ellen cannot get the PTC for her coverage in the qualified health plan because she is eligible for

Medicare.

Example 2.

The facts are the same as Example 1 , except that Ellen did not apply for the Medicare coverage by September 30. Ellen is considered eligible for government-sponsored coverage beginning on October 1. She can get the PTC for her coverage for January through September. She cannot get the PTC for her coverage in a qualified health plan as of October 1, the first day of the fourth month after she turned 65.

Exceptions. You are eligible for government-sponsored coverage under the following programs only if you are enrolled in the program.
1. A veteran's health care program listed in (5), earlier.
2. The following Tricare programs:
a. The Continued Health Care Benefit Program.
b. Retired Reserve.
c. Young Adult.
d. Reserve Select.

3. Medicaid coverage for comprehensive pregnancy-related services and CHIP coverage based on pregnancy, if the individual is enrolled in a qualified health plan at the time she becomes eligible for Medicaid or CHIP.
4. Coverage under Medicare Part A for which the individual must pay a premium.

An individual is eligible for minimum essential coverage under a Medicaid or Medicare program for which eligibility requires a determination of disability, blindness, or illness only when the responsible agency makes a favorable determination of disability.

Retroactive coverage. If APTC is being paid for coverage in a qualified health plan and you become eligible for government coverage that is effective retroactively (such as Medicaid or CHIP), you will not retroactively lose the PTC for your coverage. You can get the PTC for your coverage until the first day of the first calendar month after you are approved for the government coverage.

Example. In November, Freda enrolled in a qualified health plan for the following year and got APTC for her coverage. Freda lost her part-time job and on April 10 applied for coverage under the Medicaid program. Freda's application was approved on May 15 and Medicaid covered her medical expenses beginning April 1. For purposes of the PTC, Freda was eligible for government-sponsored coverage on June 1, the first day of the first calendar month after her application was approved. Freda can get the PTC for her coverage for January through May.

Note.
If you do not pay your premiums for Medicaid or CHIP coverage and you or a family member is terminated from the program, you cannot get the PTC for the coverage of that individual.

Employer-Sponsored Plans
The following employer-sponsored plans are MEC.
1. Group health insurance coverage for employees under:
a. A governmental plan, such as the Federal Employees Health Benefits Program.
b. A plan or coverage offered in the small or large group market within a state.
2. A self-insured group health plan for employees.
3. The Nonappropriated Fund Health Benefits Program of the Department of Defense. (This program is both government-sponsored coverage and employer-sponsored coverage.)

You are eligible for an employer-sponsored plan (and cannot get the PTC for your coverage in a qualified health plan) only if the coverage is affordable (defined later) to the employee and the coverage provides minimum value (defined later). Your family members also may be unable to get the PTC for coverage in a qualified health plan for months they were eligible to enroll in employer-sponsored coverage but only if it was affordable for the employee. If you or your family member enrolls in the employer coverage, the individual enrolled cannot get the PTC for coverage in a qualified health plan, even if the employer coverage is not affordable or does not provide minimum value.

You are not treated as eligible for employer coverage, and can get the PTC for your coverage in a qualified health plan, for a month when you cannot receive benefits under the employer coverage (for example, you are in a waiting period before the coverage becomes effective).

If you can enroll in employer coverage that is affordable and provides minimum value during an enrollment period and you do not enroll, you cannot get the PTC for your coverage in a qualified health plan for the period you could have been enrolled in the employer coverage.

Coverage after employment ends. If you are no longer employed, you are eligible for employer coverage from your former employer (for example, COBRA or retiree coverage) only for the months that you are enrolled in the employer coverage.

Individual not in your tax family. An individual who can enroll in your employer coverage who is not a member of your tax family (for example, an adult non-dependent child under age 26) is eligible for the employer coverage only for the months the individual is enrolled.

How to determine if the plan is affordable. Your employer coverage is considered affordable for you and for a family member if your share of the annual premiums for self-only coverage is not more than 9.5% of your tax family's household income for 2014.

Wellness program incentives. If you can reduce the amount of your monthly premiums by completing a wellness program incentive (such as completing a health questionnaire or attending a smoking cessation class), the amount of your premiums for purposes of determining whether your coverage is considered affordable is reduced by the amount of the incentive only if it relates to tobacco use.

Example. George can enroll in employer coverage. George's monthly premiums for self-only coverage are $450. If George, who is a smoker, attends a smoking cessation class, his monthly premiums will be reduced by $100. If George completes a cholesterol screening, his monthly premiums will be reduced by $50. Whether or not George actually completes either of these wellness program incentives, for purposes of determining whether the coverage is affordable for George, the cost of his premiums will be considered to be the amount reduced by the $100 incentive for attending a smoking cessation class but not reduced by the $50 incentive for completing a cholesterol screening. Therefore, for purposes of determining whether his coverage is considered affordable, George's monthly premium is treated as $350.

Health reimbursement arrangements. Amounts your employer contributes to a health reimbursement arrangement each year that may be used to pay premiums may count as reducing the amount you must pay for premiums. The employer also must offer another health plan.

Determining affordability at the time of enrollment. Your employer coverage is not considered affordable, if, when you enroll in a qualified health plan, the Marketplace determines that your share of the cost of your premiums for employer coverage will be more than 9.5% of what the Marketplace estimates will be your household income. Eligibility for employer coverage in this situation does not disqualify you from taking the PTC when you file your tax return, even if the actual cost of your coverage was less than 9.5% of the household income on your return. However, you will be treated as eligible for affordable employer coverage based on the household income on your tax return if:

• You did not provide current information to the Marketplace relating to your household income and the cost of your employer coverage during each annual re-enrollment period, or
• With reckless disregard for the truth you provided incorrect information to the Marketplace about your cost of premiums.

Example 1. Celia is single and has no dependents. Her household income for 2014 was $47,000. Celia's employer offered its employees a health insurance plan that required her to contribute $3,450 for selfonly coverage for 2014 (7.3% of Celia's household income). Because Celia's required contribution for self-only coverage did not exceed 9.5% of household income, her employer's plan was affordable for Celia, and if the coverage also provided minimum value, Celia was eligible for the employer coverage for all months in 2014. Celia cannot get the PTC for coverage in a qualified health plan.

Example 2. The facts are the same as in Example 1 , except that Celia is married to Jon and the employer's plan required Celia to contribute $5,300 for coverage for Celia and Jon for 2014 (11.3% of Celia's household income). Because Celia's required contribution for self-only coverage ($3,450) does not exceed 9.5% of household income, her employer's plan was affordable for Celia and Jon. Both Celia and John were eligible for the employer coverage for all months in 2014 and cannot get the PTC for coverage in a qualified health plan.

Example 3. Don was eligible to enroll in employer coverage in 2014. Don's share of the premiums was $3,700. Don applied for coverage in a qualified health plan through the Marketplace. The Marketplace projected that Don's 2014 household income would be $37,000 and determined that Don's employer coverage was unaffordable because Don's share of the premiums cost more than 9.5% of Don's household income. Don enrolled in a qualified health plan through the Marketplace with APTC and not in the employer coverage. In December, Don received an unexpected $2,500 bonus. His 2014 household income reported on his tax return was $39,500. Although Don's premiums for the employer coverage cost less than 9.5% of the household income on Don's tax return, Don is considered not eligible for the employer coverage for 2014 because the Marketplace estimated that the employer coverage would cost more than 9.5% of Don's household income. Don can get the PTC.

Example 4. Hal is eligible for employer coverage for 2014. His household income for 2014 was $33,000 and his share of premiums for self-only coverage cost $3,400, which is more than 9.5% of his household income. Hal enrolled in the employer coverage. Even though the employer coverage was not affordable, Hal cannot get the PTC for coverage in a qualified health plan because he enrolled in the employer coverage.

Example 5. Elsa is married and has 2 dependent children. Her household income for 2014 was $39,000. Elsa's employer offered only self-only coverage to employees. No family coverage was offered. The plan required Elsa to contribute $3,000 for self-only coverage for 2014 (7.7% of Elsa's household income) and provided minimum value. Because Elsa's premiums for self-only coverage cost less than 9.5% of household income, her employer's plan was affordable for Elsa. Elsa was eligible for the employer coverage and cannot get the PTC for coverage in a qualified health plan for 2014. However, because Elsa's employer did not offer coverage to Elsa's husband and children, Elsa could take the PTC for her husband and 2 children if they enrolled in a qualified health plan and otherwise qualify.

Example 6. The facts are the same as in Example 5, except that Elsa's employer also offers coverage to Elsa's husband and children. The premiums for family coverage cost $6,900 (17.7% of Elsa's household income). Because the premiums for self-only coverage cost less than 9.5% of Elsa's household income the employer coverage is considered affordable for Elsa and her family. Elsa could not take the PTC for anyone in her family.

Determining affordability for part-year period. If you are employed for part of a year or employed by different employers during the year, you determine whether your coverage is affordable by looking separately at each coverage period that is less than a full calendar year. For each period, the coverage is affordable if your share of the cost of your premiums for the entire year would not be more than 9.5% of your household income for the year.

Example. Elvis is enrolled in a qualified health plan with APTC beginning in January 2014. He begins working for a new employer in May that offers health insurance coverage with a calendar year plan year. Elvis' share of premiums for the employer coverage for the remainder of the year is $200/month, which would be $2,400 for the full plan year. Elvis informs the Marketplace of the offer of employer coverage. The Marketplace estimates that Elvis' household income for the year will be $20,000. Elvis' employer coverage is unaffordable for the period May through December because his cost for the full plan year, $2,400, would be more than 9.5% of his household income. If Elvis does not enroll in the employer plan and continues to be enrolled in a qualified health plan through the Marketplace, he will continue to be eligible for the PTC.

Coverage year not a calendar year. If your employer's coverage year is not the calendar year, you determine whether your coverage is affordable by looking separately at the coverage period in each calendar year. For each period, the coverage is affordable if what would be the total amount of your premiums if you were covered for the entire year is not more than 9.5% of your household income for the year.

Example. Maria's employer offers health insurance coverage with a plan year of September 1 – August
31. Maria's cost of premiums for the employer coverage for the period September 1, 2014 – August 31,
2015, is $3,700. Maria's household income for 2014 is $37,000. Maria's employer coverage is unaffordable for the period September 1 – December 31, 2014, because her cost for the plan year, $3,700, is more than 9.5% of her 2014 household income. If Maria enrolls in a qualified health plan for 2015 and requests APTC, the Marketplace will determine whether the employer coverage is affordable for the period January 1, 2015 – August 31,

2015, by comparing Maria's cost for the plan year, $3,700, to her estimated 2015 household income.

How to determine if a plan provides minimum value. An employer-sponsored plan provides minimum value only if the plan's share of the total allowed costs of benefits under the plan is at least 60%, that is, employees' expected cost-sharing (deductibles, co-pays, and co-insurance) under the plan is no more than 40% of the cost of the benefits. This percentage is based on actuarial principles using benefits provided to a standard population and is not based on what you actually pay for cost-sharing.

Your employer must provide you with a summary of benefits and coverage (SBC) on or before the first day of the open enrollment period for the plan you are enrolled in for the current coverage period. The employer also must provide you with SBCs you request for other plans. If you are not enrolled in a plan the employer must provide you with the SBCs for all plans in which you can enroll. The SBC will tell you whether an employer-sponsored plan provides minimum value. Beginning with coverage for 2015, your employer will send you Form 1095-C, which will tell you whether you were offered coverage in the previous year that provided minimum value (Form 1095-C, line 14).

Other Coverage Designated by the Department of Health and Human Services
The Department of Health and Human Services has designated the following health benefit plans or arrangements as minimum essential coverage.
1. Self-insured student health plans (for 2014 only).
2. State high risk pools (for 2014 only).
3. Coverage under Medicare Part C (Medicare Advantage).
4. Refugee Medical Assistance.
5. Employer coverage provided to business owners who are not employees.
6. Coverage under a group health plan provided through insurance regulated by a foreign government if:
a. A covered individual is physically absent from the U.S. for at least 1 day during the month, or
b. A covered individual is physically present in the United States for a full month and the coverage provides health benefits within the United States while the individual is on expatriate status.

In general, if you were eligible for minimum essential coverage, you are not eligible to claim the PTC for coverage through the Marketplace. However, you are treated as eligible for minimum essential coverage under a self-insured student health plan or a state high risk pool only if you are enrolled in the coverage.

Other health benefit plans that the Department of Health and Human Services designates as minimum essential coverage will be identified at irs.gov/ACA.
Records of Domestic Abuse and Abandonment

If you checked the "Relief" box in the upper right corner of Form 8962, you should keep records relating to your situation, like with all aspects of your tax return. What you have available may depend on your circumstances, however the following list provides some examples of records that may be useful. (Do not attach these records to your tax return.)

• Protective and/or restraining order.
• Police report.
• Doctor's report or letter.
• A statement from someone who was aware of, or who witnessed, the abuse or the results of the abuse. The statement should be notarized if possible.
• A statement from someone who knows of the abandonment. The statement should be notarized if possible.
Penalty Relief for Taxpayers Who Have Excess APTC

The following applies only if you have excess APTC. If you do not pay all of the tax that you owe on your 2014 return by April 15, 2015, you may be subject to a penalty for failure to pay. Even if you pay all of the tax you owe by April 15, 2015, but you did not pay enough tax during the year (through withholding from your paychecks or estimated tax payments), you may be subject to a penalty for underpayment of estimated tax. The IRS is providing relief from these penalties but not from the tax under certain circumstances if you have a balance due on your 2014 income tax return as a result of excess APTC. You will not have to pay either penalty if you meet all of the following requirements.

1. You are otherwise current with your tax filing and payment obligations. You are treated as current with your tax filing and payment obligations if, as of the date you file your 2014 income tax return, you meet both of the

following conditions:

a. You have filed, or filed an extension for, all currently required federal tax returns.
b. You paid or have entered into an installment agreement (which is not in default), an offer in compromise, or both to satisfy a federal tax liability.
2. You report the amount of excess APTC on your 2014 tax return that is timely filed, including extensions (line 46 of Form 1040, Line 29 of Form 1040A, or line 44 of Form 1040NR).
3. If you timely file your return on extension after April 15, 2015, you fully pay the underlying liability by April 15, 2016.
4. You request relief from the penalties.

If you owe a penalty for failure to pay, the IRS will send you a notice demanding payment. To request relief from the penalty for failure to pay, you should respond to the notice demanding payment of the relief from the penalty for failure to pay, you should respond to the notice demanding payment of the 9 because I received excess advance payment of the premium tax credit." The letter should be sent to the address listed in the notice demanding payment. Interest will accrue until the underlying liability is fully paid.

If you owe an estimated tax penalty, you will figure the penalty on line 79 of your Form 1040, line 51 of your Form 1040A, or line 76 of your Form 1040NR or elect to have the IRS compute the penalty for you. To request relief from the estimated tax penalty, check box A in Part II of Form 2210, complete page 1 of the form, and include the form with your return along with the statement: "Received excess advance payment of the premium tax credit." Do not attach any documentation or complete any portion of the Form 2210 other than page 1. You do not need to figure the amount of the penalty for the penalty to be waived.

More information. For more information on both of these forms of penalty relief, see Notice 2015-9 in Internal Revenue Bulletin 2015-6, available at www.irs.gov/irb/2015-6_IRB/ar12.html.
Individuals Not Lawfully Present in the United States Enrolled in a Qualified Health Plan

The PTC is not allowed for the coverage of an individual who is not lawfully present in the United States. All APTC paid for a not lawfully present individual who enrolls in a qualified health plan must be repaid. If you or a member of your family is not lawfully present and is enrolled in a qualified health plan with family members who are lawfully present for one or more months of the year, you must use the instructions under How To Determine Your Monthly Credit Amounts and How To Determine the Excess APTC That Must Be Repaid , later, to find out how much APTC, if any, you must repay. If all family members enrolled in a qualified health plan are not lawfully present, see the discussion immediately below.

All Enrolled Family Members Not Lawfully Present
If all family members enrolled in a qualified health plan are not lawfully present, all APTC must be repaid. Complete lines on Form 8962 as explained below. Leave all other lines blank.
Line 1. Complete this line according to the instructions on line 1.
Lines 2a, 3, 4, and 5. Enter -0-.

Line 9. Complete line 9 as provided in the Form 8962 instructions to determine whether you must complete Part 4 for a shared policy allocation. Complete Part 4 if instructed to do so by Table 3 of the Form 8962 instructions. Do not complete Part 5.

Line 11F (or lines 12—23, column F, if you complete Part 4). If you checked the "No" box on line 9, enter the total of your Form(s) 1095-A, Part III, line 33C, on line 11F. If you checked the "Yes" box on line 9, complete lines 12–23, column F, as provided in the Form 8962 instructions.

Lines 25, 27, and 29. Enter the amount from line 11F (or the total of lines 12–23, column F) on each line and follow the instructions on line 29.

Lawfully Present and Not Lawfully Present Family Members Enrolled
If you or a member of your family is not lawfully present and is enrolled in a qualified health plan with family members who are lawfully present for one or more months of the year, you may take the PTC only for the coverage of the lawfully present family members. You must determine and repay all APTC paid for the coverage of a not lawfully present family member. Complete Form 8962 using the following steps.

• Complete Part 1 according to the instructions. If you are instructed to repay the APTC paid for all individuals included in your tax family (for example because your household income is over 400% of the Federal poverty line), skip the rest of these steps, complete Form 8962 through line 27, and then see How To Determine the Excess APTC That Must Be Repaid , later.

• Determine your monthly credit amounts using the instructions under How To Determine Your Monthly Credit Amounts , later.
• Complete line 9, including Parts 4 and 5 if instructed to do so.

• Check the "No" box on line 10, skip line 11, and complete lines 12–25. If line 24 is less than line 25, you have excess APTC. See How To Determine the Excess APTC That Must Be Repaid , later. If line 24 is equal to or greater than line 25, complete line 26 as instructed (do not follow the instructions under How To Determine the Excess APTC That Must Be Repaid).

How To Determine Your Monthly Credit Amounts

If the only changes in enrollment involved your not lawfully present family member(s), see Not lawfully present family members disenrolled and no other changes in enrollment or coverage family next. If there were other changes in enrollment (lawfully present individuals starting or stopping coverage) or in your coverage family (see the instructions for Form 8962) in addition to disenrollment of your not lawfully present family member(s), see Changes in enrollment or coverage family involving a lawfully present family member below. If a not lawfully present family member was enrolled for the entire year, see No reference month , later.

Not lawfully present family members disenrolled and no other changes in enrollment or coverage family. If all of your family members who are not lawfully present are enrolled for only a portion of the year and there are no other changes during the year in your coverage family or the family members who are enrolled in the coverage, you should enter on Form 8962 for every month of the year the enrollment premiums and applicable SLCSP premium the Marketplace reports on Form 1095-A for the months when only lawfully present individuals were enrolled in the coverage.

Example 1. Andrew enrolls himself and his three dependents, Terri, Phil and Anne in a qualified health plan. Anne is not lawfully present in the United States. The monthly enrollment premiums for the plan are $1,000. No one in Andrew's family is eligible for minimum essential coverage (other than Marketplace coverage) and the applicable SLCSP premium that would apply to all four members of Andrew's family is $1,200. There are no changes in the coverage family during the year. Anne is disenrolled from coverage as of April 1. The monthly enrollment premiums for Andrew and his other two dependents are $800 and the applicable SLCSP premium that applies to Andrew's coverage family of 3 is $900. The Marketplace reports the following amounts on Form 1095-A, Part III.

Months Column A Column B
January, February, March $1,000 $1,200
April through December 800 900
When completing Form 8962, Andrew enters $800 as the enrollment premiums on lines 12–23, column A, and $900 as the premium for the applicable SLCSP on lines 12–23, column B.

Changes in enrollment or coverage family involving a lawfully present family member. If your not lawfully present family members are enrolled for only a portion of the year and there are other enrollment changes or changes in your coverage family, use these rules to determine the enrollment premiums and the applicable SLCSP premium for the months any not lawfully present family members are enrolled. First, use Worksheet A, later, to determine if you have a reference month for enrollment premiums or for the applicable SLCSP premium. You may have a reference month for enrollment premiums (discussed next) or a reference month for the applicable SLCSP premium (discussed below), or for both.

Reference month for enrollment premiums. A reference month for enrollment premiums is a month in which the not lawfully present family member is not enrolled in coverage and there are no other changes in the members of your family who are enrolled in the coverage. In other words, your enrolled family members are the same during the reference month as for a month the not lawfully present member was enrolled, except that the not lawfully present family member is not enrolled. Enter on Form 8962, Part 2, column A, the enrollment premiums for the reference month as the enrollment premiums for the months the not lawfully present family member was enrolled.

Reference month for SLCSP premium. A reference month for the applicable SLCSP premium is a month in which the not lawfully present family member is not enrolled in coverage and there are no other changes in your coverage family. In other words, your coverage family is the same during the reference month as for a month the not lawfully present family member was enrolled, except the not lawfully present family member is not included in your coverage family. Enter on Form 8962, Part 2, column B, the applicable SLCSP premium for the reference month as the applicable SLCSP premium for the months the not lawfully present family member was enrolled.

No reference month. If you do not have a reference month for enrollment premiums, you may have to contact your insurance company to find out what the amount of the enrollment premiums would have been if the policy had covered only lawfully present family members. If you do not have a reference month for the applicable SLCSP premium, you must look up the SLCSP premium that applies to your coverage family (without any not lawfully present family members). See Determining the Premium for the Applicable Second Lowest Cost Silver Plan (SLCSP) , later.
You may use Worksheet A, later, to determine whether or not you have any reference months.

Example 2. The facts are the same as in Example 1 , earlier, except that Andrew becomes eligible for employer-sponsored coverage on September 1, notifies the Marketplace, but remains enrolled in the qualified health plan (although he cannot take the premium tax credit for his coverage for the months after August). The applicable SLCSP premium that applies to Terri and Phil only is $400. The Marketplace reports the following amounts on Form 1095-A, Part III.

Months Column A Column B
January, February, March $1,000 $1,200
April through August 800 900
September through December 800 400

Andrew cannot use line 11 and must complete lines 12–23 on Form 8962. April through August are reference months for both enrollment premiums and the applicable SLCSP premium for January through March (the months Anne was enrolled in coverage) because Andrew's coverage family and enrolled family members for April through August (Andrew, Phil and Terri) are the same as for January through March except for Anne who is not lawfully present. (September through December are also reference months for enrollment premiums.) The enrollment premiums and SLCSP premium for April through August are the same amounts they would have been for

January through March without Anne. Therefore, for the months January through March, Andrew enters on Form 8962, lines 12–23, $800 (the enrollment premiums for April through August) in column A and $900 (the SLCSP premium that applies to the coverage family for April through August) in column B.

Example 3. The facts are the same as in Example 1 , earlier, except that Andrew becomes eligible for employer-sponsored coverage on April 1, notifies the Marketplace, but remains enrolled in the qualified health plan. The Marketplace reports the following amounts on Form 1095-A, Part III.

Months Column A Column B
January, February, March $1,000 $1,200
April through December 800 400

Andrew does not have a reference month for the applicable SLCSP premium for the months Anne was enrolled in the qualified health plan because there is another change in his coverage family for the months April through December (Andrew is not in the coverage family because he is eligible for employer-sponsored coverage). Thus, there are no months when Andrew's coverage family is the same (except for Anne) before and after Anne is disenrolled from coverage. Andrew must look up the SLCSP premium that applies to his coverage family without Anne. Andrew determines that the correct applicable SLCSP premium to enter on Form 8962 for the months January through March for a coverage family consisting of Andrew, Terri, and Phil is $900.

April through December are reference months for Andrew for enrollment premiums because the family members who are enrolled for those months are the same family members who were enrolled in January through March, except for Anne.

Therefore, for the months January through March, Andrew enters on Form 8962, lines 12–23, $800 (the enrollment premiums for April through December) in column A and $900 (the SLCSP premium that would apply to the coverage family of Andrew, Terri, and Phil) in column B.

Worksheet A. Do You Have Any Reference Months?
Note. Use this worksheet to determine whether or not you have any reference months.

Months in 2014 Jan. Feb. Mar. Apr. May Jun. Jul. Aug. Sep. Oct. Nov. Dec.
1. Check a box for each month in which any family members not lawfully present were enrolled in coverage ❑ ❑ ❑ ❑ ❑ ❑ ❑ ❑ ❑ ❑ ❑ ❑
2. Check a box for each month in which:
• Only lawfully present family members were enrolled in coverage, and
• There were no other changes in members of your tax family who are enrolled in coverage, as compared to a month for which you checked a box on line 1 ❑ ❑ ❑ ❑ ❑ ❑ ❑ ❑ ❑ ❑ ❑ ❑

The months for which you checked boxes on line 2 are your reference months for enrollment premiums. Use the enrollment premium reported on Form 1095-A, Part III, column A, for the reference month as your enrollment premium on Form 8962 for the month(s) you checked on line 1.

Note. If you did not check any boxes on this line, see No reference month , earlier.
3. Check a box for each month in which:
• Only lawfully present family members were enrolled in coverage, and
• There were no other changes in your coverage family, as compared to a month for which you checked a box on line 1 ❑ ❑ ❑ ❑ ❑ ❑ ❑ ❑ ❑ ❑ ❑ ❑

The months for which you checked boxes on line 3 are your reference months for the applicable SLCSP premium. Use the applicable SLCSP premium reported on Form 1095-A, Part III, column B, for the reference month as your applicable SLCSP premium on Form 8962 for the month(s) you checked on line 1.

Note. If you did not check any boxes on this line, see No reference month , earlier.
How To Determine the Excess APTC That Must Be Repaid

The excess APTC repayment limitation (see the instructions for Form 8962, line 28) applies only to excess APTC for coverage of lawfully present individuals. Excess APTC that relates to the coverage of individuals who are not lawfully present must be repaid without limitation. Use Worksheet B, later, to determine the amount of excess APTC that you must repay if all of the following apply.

• You or a member of your family is not lawfully present and is enrolled in a

qualified health plan with family members who are lawfully present for one or more months of the year.
• You have excess APTC on line 27 of Form 8962.
• Your excess APTC on line 27 of Form 8962 is more than your repayment limitation amount from Table 5 in the Form 8962 instructions.

If line 27 is not more than your repayment limitation amount from Table 5 in the Form 8962 instructions, do not complete Worksheet B. Leave line 28 of Form 8962 blank, enter the amount from line 27 on line 29, and follow the instructions on line 29. If you must complete Worksheet B, see the illustrated example next.

Illustrated Example of Determining the Excess APTC That Must Be Repaid

Andrew enrolls himself and his three dependents, Terri, Phil, and Anne in a qualified health plan. Anne is not lawfully present in the United States and is disenrolled from the coverage as of April 1. Andrew becomes eligible for employer-sponsored coverage on September 1, notifies the Marketplace, but remains enrolled in the qualified health plan. When Andrew and his family enroll in the qualified health plan, the Marketplace estimates that their household income will be $47,100, which is 200% of the Federal poverty line. The annual contribution amount based on this estimate used to determine APTC is $2,967 or $247 per month. The Marketplace reports the following amounts on Form 1095-A, Part III.

| Months | Column A | Column B | Column C |
|---|---|---|---|
| January, February, March | $1,000 | $1,200 | $953 |
| April through August | 800 | 900 | 653 |
| September through December | 800 | 400 | 153 |

Andrew's household income for the year on his Form 8962, line 3, is $58,875, which is 250% of the Federal poverty line. The annual contribution amount Andrew enters on line 8a is $4,739 and the monthly contribution amount he enters on line 8b is $395.

April through August are reference months for both enrollment premiums and the applicable SLCSP premium for January through March (the months Anne was enrolled in coverage) because Andrew's coverage family and enrolled family members for April through August (Andrew, Phil and Terri) are the same as for January through March except for Anne. (September through December are also reference months for enrollment premiums.) Therefore, for the months January through March, Andrew enters on Form 8962, lines 12–23, $800 (the enrollment premiums for April through August) in column A and $900 (the SLCSP premium that applies to the coverage family for April through August) in column B.

Andrew's PTC on line 24 is $4,060, his APTC on line 25 is $6,736, and his excess APTC on line 27 is $2,676. Andrew files his tax return using the head-of-household filing status. Andrew's Table 5 repayment limitation amount is $1,500. Because Andrew's line 27 is more than his repayment limitation amount, he computes the amount of excess APTC he must repay by completing Worksheet B as shown later.

Worksheet B. Excess APTC That Must Be Repaid

Note. Complete columns only for the months a not lawfully present family member was enrolled in coverage. (If you completed Worksheet A, earlier, these are the months for which you checked a box on line 1 of the worksheet.)

Months in 2014 Jan Feb Mar Apr May Jun Jul Aug Sep Oct Nov Dec
1. Enter APTC from Form 1095-A, Part III, column C . . . . . .
2. Enter the monthly credit amount from Form 8962, Part 2, column E
3. Subtract line 2 from line 1. If zero or less, leave this line blank and skip lines 4–10 for the month
4. Enter the monthly premium amount from Form 1095-A, Part III, column A . .
5. Enter the SLCSP premium from Form 1095-A, Part III, column B . . . . . .
6. Enter the monthly contribution amount from Form 8962, line 8b . . . . . 7. Subtract line 6 from line 5
8. Enter the smaller of line 4 or line 7 . . . . .
9. Subtract line 8 from line 1. If zero or less, enter -0- . . . . .
10. Subtract line 9 from line 3

11. Add the amounts on line 10. If all of your line 3 results were zero or less, stop here. None of your excess APTC was from individuals who were not lawfully present. Enter the repayment limitation from Table 5 in the Form 8962 instructions on Form 8962, line 28, and continue to line 29

11.

12. Enter the repayment limitation from Table 5 in the Form 8962 instructions 12.

13. Add lines 11 and 12 13.

14. Enter the amount from Form 8962, line 27 14.

15. Compare lines 13 and 14.

• If line 14 is more than line 13, enter the amount from line 13 on Form 8962, lines 28 and 29 and follow the instructions on line 29.

• If line 14 is less than or equal to line 13, leave Form 8962, line 28, blank and enter the amount from line 27 on line 29.

Andrew's Worksheet B. Excess APTC That Must Be Repaid Note. Complete columns only for the months a not lawfully present family member was enrolled in coverage. (If you completed Worksheet A, earlier, these are the months for which you checked a box on line 1 of the worksheet.)

Months in 2014 Jan Feb Mar Apr May Jun Jul Aug Sep Oct Nov Dec

1. Enter APTC from Form 1095-A, Part III, column C . . . . . . $953 $953 $953

2. Enter the monthly credit amount from Form 8962, Part 2, column E 505 505 505

3. Subtract line 2 from line 1. If zero or less, leave this line blank and skip lines 4–10 for the month 448 448 448

4. Enter the monthly premium amount from Form 1095-A, Part III, column A . . 1,000 1,000 1,000

5. Enter the SLCSP premium from Form 1095-A, Part III, column B . . . . . . 1,200 1,200 1,200

6. Enter the monthly contribution amount from Form 8962, line 8b . . . . . 395 395 395

7. Subtract line 6 from line 5 805 805 805

8. Enter the smaller of line 4 or line 7 . . . . . 805 805 805

9. Subtract line 8 from line 1. If zero or less, enter -0- . . . . . 148 148 148

10. Subtract line 9 from line 3 300 300 300

11. Add the amounts on line 10. If all of your line 3 results were zero or less, stop here. None of your excess APTC was from individuals who were not lawfully present. Enter the repayment limitation from Table 5 in the Form 8962 instructions on Form 8962, line 28, and continue to line 29

11. 900

12. Enter the repayment limitation from Table 5 in the Form 8962 instructions 12. 1,500

13. Add lines 11 and 12 13. 2,400 14. Enter the amount from Form 8962, line 27 14. 2,676

15. Compare lines 13 and 14.

• If line 14 is more than line 13, enter the amount from line 13 on Form 8962, lines 28 and 29 and follow the instructions on line 29.

• If line 14 is less than or equal to line 13, leave Form 8962, line 28, blank and enter the amount from line 27 on line 29.

Andrew's Worksheet B

Line 1. Andrew enters $953. This is the monthly APTC shown on Form 1095-A, Part III, column C for January, February, and March (the months that Anne was enrolled in coverage).

Line 2. Andrew enters $505. This is the amount from Form 8962, Part 2, Column E, for January – March and represents the applicable monthly SLCSP premium for April – August (reference months for the applicable SLCSP premium) for Andrew, Terri, and Phil of $900 minus the monthly contribution amount of $395 from Form 8962, line 8b.

Line 4. Line 4. A, Part III, column A.

Line 5. Andrew enters $1,200. This is the applicable SLCSP premium shown on Form 1095-A, Part III, column B.

Line 6. Andrew enters $395. This is the monthly contribution amount from Form 8962, line 8b.

Lines 7–14. Andrew completes these lines as instructed on Worksheet B.

Line 15. Line 14 is more than line 13. Accordingly, Andrew enters the amount from line 13 ($2,400) on Form 8962, lines 28 and 29.

Individuals Filing a Tax Return and Claiming No Personal Exemptions

If you file an income tax return but claim no personal exemptions, even for yourself, your tax family size is 0 and you cannot take the PTC. You must repay the APTC for which you are responsible. Complete lines on Form 8962 as explained below. Leave all other lines blank.

Note.

If you enrolled yourself or another person in a qualified health plan and APTC was paid for the coverage, the taxpayer claiming a personal exemption for the person enrolled must reconcile the APTC. See Policy shared with an individual for whom another taxpayer claims a personal exemption in Part 4 of the Form 8962 instructions. If you enrolled only yourself and another taxpayer claims you as a dependent, you do not have to file Form 8962. If you enrolled yourself or another person and no one else claims a personal exemption for the person enrolled, you must file Form 8962 and reconcile the APTC. Lines 1, 2a, 3, 4, and 5. Enter -0-.

Line 9. Complete line 9 as provided in the Form 8962 instructions to determine whether you must complete Part 4 for a shared policy allocation. Complete Part 4 if instructed to do so by Table 3 of the Form 8962 instructions. Do not complete Part 5.

Line 11F (or lines 12–23, column F, if you complete Part 4). If you checked the "No" box on line 9, enter the total of your Form(s) 1095-A, Part III, line 33C, on line 11F. If you checked the "Yes" box on line 9, complete lines 12–23, column F, as provided in the Form 8962 instructions.

Lines 25, 27, and 29. Enter the amount from line 11F (or the total of lines 12–23, column F) on each line and follow the instructions on line 29.

Example 1. Jeff enrolls himself in a qualified health plan for 2014. The Form 1095-A he received from the Marketplace shows that APTC of $4,000 was paid for his coverage. Jeff files an income tax return on Form 1040A for 2014 and claims no personal exemptions. Jeff completes Form 8962 as follows.

Lines 1, 2a, 3, 4, and 5. Jeff enters -0-.
Line 9. Jeff checks the "No" box.
Lines 11F, 25, 27, and 29. Jeff enters $4,000 APTC on these lines and on line 29 of his Form 1040A.

Example 2. Mark enrolls himself and his child, Donna, in a qualified health plan with coverage effective for all of 2014. The Form 1095-A he received from the Marketplace shows that $6,000 of APTC was paid for their coverage ($500 is entered in Part III, column C, for each of lines 21–32). Mark files an income tax return for 2014 on Form 1040 and claims no personal exemptions. Mark's parents, Steve and Sherry, claim a personal exemption for Mark. No one claims a personal exemption for Donna. Because Mark enrolled Donna in coverage and no one claims a personal exemption for Donna, Mark must reconcile the APTC paid for Donna's coverage. Steve and Sherry must reconcile the APTC paid for Mark's coverage. Because Steve and Sherry must reconcile the APTC paid for Mark's coverage and Mark must reconcile the APTC paid for Donna's coverage, Mark must complete Part 4 of Form 8962 to allocate shared policy amounts with Steve and Sherry. Mark, Sherry, and Steve do not agree on an allocation percentage. Mark completes Form 8962 as follows.

Lines 1, 2a, 3, 4, and 5. Mark enters -0-.
Line 9. Mark answers "Yes" to questions 3a and 3b on Table 3 in the Form 8962 instructions. He checks the "Yes" box on line 9 as instructed by his answer to question 3b.

Line 30 (Part 4). Mark enters the Marketplace assigned policy number in column a, Steve's social security number in column b, "01" in column c, and "12" in column d. He leaves columns e and f blank because he is not an applicable taxpayer. He enters "0.50" in column g. This is the allocation percentage based on the rules under Policy shared with an individual for whom another taxpayer claims a personal exemption in the Form 8962 instructions.
exemption in the Form 8962 instructions.
A).

Lines 25, 27, and 29. Mark enters $3,000 APTC, which is the total of lines 12–23, column F, on these lines and on line 46 of his Form 1040.
Determining the Premium for the Applicable Second Lowest Cost Silver Plan (SLCSP)

If you or a member of your family enrolls in a qualified health plan and requests financial assistance, the Marketplace identifies the SLCSP premium that applies to your coverage family, based on information you provided on the application, and reports this amount on Form 1095-A. The Marketplace determines the applicable SLCSP premium based on your address and the members of your coverage family. Providing correct information on your application for financial assistance and notifying the Marketplace if you move or the members of your coverage family change is necessary for the Marketplace to report a correct applicable SLCSP premium. If the Marketplace does not have accurate and updated information, the applicable SLCSP premium the Marketplace reports on Form 1095-A may not be accurate for all months and you will need to determine the correct applicable

SLCSP premium for those months.

If you did not request financial assistance, the Marketplace may not report an applicable SLCSP premium (Part III, column B, will be blank), or it may report an SLCSP premium that applies to everyone enrolled in your qualified health plan because it may not be able to identify the members of your coverage family from the information on your application. If you take the PTC on your tax return, you will need to determine the SLCSP premium that applies to your coverage family for each month of coverage.

Only the Marketplaces are able to provide SLCSP premiums. The Federally-facilitated Marketplace and most state Marketplaces have provided SLCSP premium tools which, as you prepare your tax return, you may use to look up the SLCSP premium that applies to your coverage family for each month. If you enrolled through the Federally-facilitated Marketplace you will find the tool at
https://www.healthcare.gov/taxes/tools/silver/.

If you enrolled through a state Marketplace, you may find information about whether your state has an SLCSP premium tool on that state's website. If your state Marketplace does not have an SLCSP premium tool, you will need to contact the state Marketplace for the correct SLCSP premium.

Shared Policy Allocation
This section covers multiple allocations of policy amounts.

Before you read this section, first read Part 4–Shared Policy Allocation in the Form 8962 instructions. Then use the following instructions to complete Part 4 of Form 8962 if one qualified health plan covers individuals from three or more tax families in the same month. Specifically, these instructions apply to:

• Taxpayers who must allocate policy amounts because of a divorce or legal separation in 2014 and also must allocate policy amounts with another taxpayer (for example, a grandparent who claims the personal exemption amount for a child enrolled with the former spouses).
• Taxpayers who must allocate policy amounts because they are legally married but are not filing a joint return (for example, filing their returns as married filing separately), and also must allocate policy amounts with another taxpayer (for example, a grandparent who claims the personal exemption amount for a child enrolled with the spouses).

• Three or more taxpayers who are claiming personal exemptions for individuals enrolled together in a qualified health plan.
Note.

As explained in the Form 8962 instructions, you must allocate enrollment premiums with another tax family if you and the other tax family enrolled in a qualified health plan as two tax families, remained two separate tax families for the entire year, and either (1) only one Form 1095-A was received for the plan, or (2) the information on the Form 1095-A, Part III, column B is incorrect for any family for any month. See Policy shared by two or more tax families in the instructions for Form 8962 instructions for more information. If you must also perform this allocation of enrollment premiums and another allocation of policy amounts, complete the enrollment premium allocation for a policy shared by two or more tax families first and then perform the second allocation.

Taxpayers Allocating Policy Amounts as Divorced or Legally Separated in 2014 and Because Individuals Enrolled With a Spouse's Tax Family Are Claimed By Another Taxpayer
Use this section to allocate policy amounts from a qualified health plan if you meet either of the following conditions and no other allocations for the policy are necessary.

• You are allocating amounts with a former spouse as a result of your divorce or legal separation in 2014 and also are allocating amounts with another taxpayer who is claiming a personal exemption for an individual who, when you were married to the former spouse, was enrolled in a qualified health plan with members of your and your former spouse's tax families.

• You are the taxpayer who is claiming a personal exemption for an individual enrolled in the plan with tax family members of taxpayers who also must allocate policy amounts as a result of divorce or separation in 2014.

Example. Kara and David and their two children, Meredith and Sam, enroll in a qualified health plan for 2014. Kara and David were married at the beginning of 2014 and divorce in 2014. Meredith and Sam move in with their grandmother, Lydia, in May of 2014. Lydia claims Meredith and Sam as dependents on her 2014 income tax return. Kara, David, and Lydia use this section to allocate policy amounts to compute their respective PTC and reconcile PTC with the APTC paid.

Kara and David use the allocation method under Taxpayers Allocating Due to a 2014 Divorce or Legal Separation and Also Allocating With Another Taxpayer , next.

Lydia uses the allocation method under Taxpayer Allocating With Taxpayers Who Divorced or Legally Separated in 2014 , later.

## Taxpayers Allocating Due to a 2014 Divorce or Legal Separation and Also Allocating With Another Taxpayer

Use this allocation method if you divorced or legally separated during the year and you must allocate policy amounts with your former spouse as well as with another taxpayer claiming a personal exemption for an individual enrolled in a qualified health plan with members of your and your former spouse's tax families.

Step 1. Determine an allocation percentage with your former spouse. You use this percentage to allocate the total enrollment premiums, the applicable SLCSP premiums, and APTC for coverage under the plan during the months you were married. You will find these amounts on your Form(s) 1095-A, Part III, columns A, B, and C, respectively. You and your former spouse can allocate these amounts using any percentage you agree on between zero and one hundred percent, but you must allocate all amounts using the same percentage. If you do not agree on a percentage, you and your former spouse must allocate 50% of each of these amounts to each of you.

Step 2. Separately from the first allocation, determine an allocation percentage with the taxpayer(s) claiming the personal exemption(s) for the individual(s) enrolled in the plan with a member of your tax family or a member of your former spouse's tax family. You may agree on any allocation percentage between zero and one hundred percent. You may use the percentage you agreed on for every month that this allocation rule applies, or you may agree on different percentages for different months. However, you must use the same allocation percentage for all policy amounts (enrollment premiums, applicable SLCSP premiums, and APTC) in a month. If you cannot agree on an allocation percentage, the allocation percentage is equal to the number of individuals for whom the other taxpayer claims a personal exemption for the tax year who were enrolled in the plan for which you are allocating policy amounts, divided by the total number of individuals enrolled in the qualified health plan. The allocation percentage is the percentage that applies to the amounts the taxpayer claiming the personal exemption must use to compute PTC and reconcile it with APTC. You and your former spouse must compute PTC and reconcile APTC using the remaining amounts.

Step 3. Complete Worksheet C below.
Worksheet C. Allocations for the Divorced or Legally Separated Taxpayers
1. Enter as a decimal your percentage from Step 1 above 1.
2. Enter 1.0. 2. 1.0
3. Enter as a decimal the total of the percentage(s) from Step 2 above allocated to the other taxpayer(s).
Note. See Example 2 later for details on adding the percentages for multiple taxpayers 3.

4. Subtract line 3 from line 2 4.
5. Multiply line 1 by line 4. Enter the result as a decimal. This is your allocation percentage. Go to Step 4 below 5.

Step 4. If you use the same percentage in Step 2 above for every month to which this allocation method applies, use only one of lines 30-33 in Part 4 to report the allocation. If you use different percentages for different months under Step 2, use a separate line in Part 4 for each allocation percentage. Complete the line as explained below.

Column a. Enter the Marketplace-assigned policy number from Form 1095-A, line 2. If the policy number on the Form 1095-A is more than 15 characters, enter only the last 15 characters.
Column b. Enter the SSN of your former spouse.
Column c. Enter the first month you are allocating policy amounts. For example, if you are allocating a percentage from January through June, enter "01" in column c.
Column d. Enter the last month you are allocating policy amounts. For example, if you are allocating a percentage from January through June, enter "06" in column d.
Column e. Enter the decimal from Worksheet C, line 5.
Column f. If APTC was paid, enter the decimal from Worksheet C, line 5. If no APTC was paid, enter the decimal from Worksheet C, line 1.
Column g. If APTC was paid, enter the decimal from Worksheet C, line 5. If

no APTC was paid, leave this column blank.

Taxpayer Allocating With Taxpayers Who Divorced or Legally Separated in 2014

Use this allocation method if you are claiming the personal exemption for one or more individuals who were enrolled in a qualified health plan with members of the tax families of taxpayers who also must allocate policy amounts as a result of divorce or legal separation in 2014. If no APTC was paid, allocate only the enrollment premiums. You must look up the applicable SLCSP premium. See Determining the Premium for the Applicable Second Lowest Cost Silver Plan (SLCSP), earlier.

Step 1. Determine an allocation percentage with one of the former spouses. You may agree on any allocation percentage between zero and one hundred percent. You may use the percentage you agreed on for every month during which this allocation rule applies, or you may agree on different percentages for different months. However, you must use the same allocation percentage for all policy amounts (enrollment premiums, applicable SLCSP premiums, and APTC) in a month. If you cannot agree on an allocation percentage, the allocation percentage is equal to the number of individuals for whom you claim a personal exemption for the tax year who were enrolled in the qualified health plan for which you are allocating policy amounts, divided by the total number of individuals enrolled in the plan. The allocation percentage is the percentage that applies to the amounts you must use to compute PTC and reconcile it with APTC. The former spouse must compute PTC and reconcile APTC using the remaining amounts.

Step 2. Allocate the policy amounts with the second former spouse using the same rules as Step 1 above. Enter the percentage on line 4 of Worksheet D.

Step 3. Complete Worksheet D below.

Worksheet D. Taxpayer Allocating with Divorced or Separated Taxpayers

1. Enter the decimal from line 1 of the Worksheet C completed by one of the former spouses from Step 1 above 1.

2. Enter as a decimal the percentage from Step 1 above 2.

3. Multiply line 1 by line 2 3.

4. Enter the decimal from line 1 of the Worksheet C completed by the other former spouse from Step 2 above 4.

5. Enter as a decimal the percentage from Step 2 above 5.

6. Multiply line 4 by line 5 6.

7. Add line 3 and line 6. This is the allocation percentage. Go to Step 4 below
7.

Step 4. If you use the same percentages in Steps 1 and 2 above for every month to which this allocation method applies, use only one of lines 30-33 in Part 4 to report the allocation. If you use different percentages for different months in Step 1 or Step 2, use a separate line in Part 4 for each allocation percentage. Complete the line as explained below.

Column a. Enter the Marketplace-assigned policy number from Form 1095-A, line 2. If the policy number on the Form 1095-A is more than 15 characters, enter only the last 15 characters.
Column b. Enter the SSN of the former spouse whose percentage you entered in Worksheet D, line 1.
Column c. Enter the first month you are allocating policy amounts. For example, if you are allocating a percentage from January through June, enter "01" in column c.
Column d. Enter the last month you are allocating policy amounts. For example, if you are allocating a percentage from January through June, enter "06" in column d.
Column e. Enter the decimal from Worksheet D, line 7.

Columns f and g. If APTC was paid, enter the decimal from Worksheet D, line 7. If no APTC was paid, leave these columns blank.
Example 1. Kara and David were married at the beginning of 2014 and have two children, Meredith and Sam. Kara enrolled herself, David, Meredith, and Sam in a qualified health plan with coverage effective January 1. For each month of coverage the enrollment premiums were $700, the applicable SLCSP premium for a coverage family of four was $650, and the APTC was $425.

Meredith and Sam moved in with their grandmother, Lydia, in May. Kara and David divorced in September. Kara enrolled in a new qualified health plan for self-only coverage. David became eligible for and enrolled in employer-sponsored self-only coverage. Meredith and Sam became eligible for and enrolled in government-sponsored coverage. All of the new plans have coverage effective October 1. Lydia is enrolled in employer-sponsored coverage.

On their respective tax returns, Kara files as single and claims only her own personal exemption, David files as single and claims only his own personal exemption, and Lydia files as head of household and claims personal exemptions for Meredith and Sam.

Under Step 1 of Taxpayers Allocating Due to a 2014 Divorce or Legal Separation and Also Allocating With Another Taxpayer , Kara and David agree to allocate the policy amounts 30% to Kara and 70% to David. Under Step 2 of that method (Kara, David) and under the method for Taxpayer Allocating With Taxpayers Who Divorced or Legally Separated in 2014 (Lydia), Kara and Lydia agree to allocate 80% of the policy amounts to Lydia, and David and Lydia agree to allocate 50% of the policy amounts to Lydia. Each of them completes a worksheet as shown below and uses it to complete Part 4.

Kara completes Worksheet C as follows.
Kara's Worksheet C. Allocations for Divorced or Legally Separated Taxpayers
1. Enter as a decimal your percentage from Step 1 above 1. .30
2. Enter 1.0 2. 1.0
3. Enter as a decimal the total of the percentages from Step 2 above allocated to the other taxpayer(s) 3. .80
4. Subtract line 3 from line 2 4. .20
5. Multiply line 1 by line 4. Enter the result as a decimal. This is the allocation percentage. Go to Step 4 below 5. .06
After completing Worksheet C, Kara completes Form 8962, Part 4, line 30, as follows.
Column a. Kara enters the Marketplace-assigned policy number from Form 1095-A, line 2.
Column b. Kara enters David's SSN.
Column c. Kara enters "01."
Column d. Kara enters "09." Columns e, f, and g. Kara enters "0.06."

After completing Part 4, Kara multiplies the amounts from Form 1095-A, Part III, by the corresponding percentages in Part 4, and enters these allocated amounts on Form 8962, lines 12-20, columns A, B, and F. On each of those lines she will enter $42 in column A (enrollment premiums of $700 x 0.06), $39 in column B (applicable SLCSP premium of $650 x 0.06), and $26 in column F (APTC of $425 x 0.06). She completes her Form 8962, lines 21-23, columns A, B, and F, by entering the monthly amounts from her separate Form 1095-A for her self-only coverage from October through December. She does not allocate those amounts.

David completes Worksheet C as follows.
David's Worksheet C. Allocations for Divorced or Legally Separated Taxpayer
1. Enter as a decimal your percentage from Step 1 above 1. .70
2. Enter 1.0 2. 1.0
3. Enter as a decimal the total of the percentages from Step 2 above allocated to the other taxpayer(s) 3. .50
4. Subtract line 3 from line 2 4. .50
5. Multiply line 1 by line 4. Enter the result as a decimal. This is the allocation percentage. Go to Step 4 below 5. .35
After completing Worksheet C, David completes Form 8962, Part 4, line 30, as follows.
Column a. David enters the Marketplace-assigned policy number from Form 1095-A, line 2.
Column b. David enters Kara's SSN.
Column c. David enters "01."
Column d. David enters "09."
Columns e, f, and g. David enters "0.35."

After completing Part 4, David multiplies the amounts from Form 1095-A, Part III, by the corresponding percentages in Part 4, and enters these allocated amounts on Form 8962, lines 12-20, columns A, B, and F. On each of those lines he will enter $245 in column A (enrollment premiums of $700 x 0.35), $228 in column B (applicable SLCSP premium of $650 x 0.35), and $149 in column F (APTC of $425 x 0.35). David leaves Form 8962, lines 21-23 blank because he was not enrolled in a qualified health plan during October through December.

Lydia completes Worksheet D as follows.

Lydia's Worksheet D. Taxpayer Allocating with Divorced or Legally Separated Taxpayers 1. Enter the decimal from line 1 of the Worksheet C completed by the former spouse from Step 1 above 1. .30

2. Enter as a decimal the percentage from Step 1 above 2. .80

3. Multiply line 1 by line 2.3. .24
4. Enter the decimal from line 1 of the Worksheet C completed by the other former spouse from Step 2 above 4. .70
5. Enter as a decimal the percentage from Step 2 above 5. .50
6. Multiply line 4 by line 5 6. .35
7. Add line 3 and line 6. This is the allocation percentage. Go to Step 4 below 7. .59

After completing Worksheet D, Lydia completes Form 8962, Part 4, line 30, as follows.

Column a. Lydia enters the Marketplace-assigned policy number from Form 1095-A, line 2.

Column b. Lydia enters Kara's SSN.

Column c. Lydia enters "01."

Column d. Lydia enters "09."

Columns e, f, and g. Lydia enters "0.59."

After completing Part 4, Lydia multiplies the amounts from Form 1095-A, Part III, by the corresponding percentages in Part 4, and enters these allocated amounts on Form 8962, lines 12-20, columns A, B, and F. On each of those lines she will enter $413 in column A (enrollment premiums of $700 x 0.59), $384 in column B (applicable SLCSP premium of $650 x 0.59), and $251 in column F (APTC of $425 x 0.59). Lydia leaves Form 8962, lines 21-23 blank because she, Meredith, and Sam were not enrolled in a qualified health plan during October through December.

Example 2. The facts are the same as Example 1 except that in May, Meredith moved in with her grandmother, Lydia, and Sam moved in with his aunt, Kimberly.

On their respective tax returns, Kara files as single and claims only her own personal exemption, David files as single and claims only his own personal exemption, Lydia files as head of household and claims Meredith's personal exemption, and Kimberly files as head of household and claims Sam's personal exemption.

Under Step 1 of Taxpayers Allocating Due to a 2014 Divorce or Legal Separation and Also Allocating With Another Taxpayer , Kara and David agree to allocate the policy amounts 40% to Kara and 60% to David. Under Step 2 of that method (Kara, David) and under the method for Taxpayer

Allocating With Taxpayers Who Divorced or Legally Separated in 2014 (Lydia, Kimberly), Kara and Lydia agree to allocate 50% of the policy amounts to Lydia, and Kara and Kimberly agree to allocate 25% of the policy amounts to Kimberly. David and Lydia agree to allocate 20% of the policy amounts to Lydia, and David and Kimberly agree to allocate 25% of the policy amounts to Kimberly. Each of them completes a worksheet as shown below and uses it to complete Part 4.

Kara completes Worksheet C as follows.
Kara's Worksheet C. Allocations for Divorced or Legally Separated Taxpayer
1. Enter as a decimal your percentage from Step 1 above 1. .40
2. Enter 1.0 2. 1.0
3. Enter as a decimal the total of the percentages from Step 2 above allocated to the other taxpayer(s) 3. .75*
4. Subtract line 3 from line 2 4. .25
5. Multiply line 1 by line 4. Enter the result as a decimal. This is the allocation percentage. Go to Step 4 below 5. .10
*This is the total of Kara's agreed percentages with Lydia and Kimberly (.50 + .25).
After completing Worksheet C, Kara completes Form 8962, Part 4, line 30, as follows.
Column a. Kara enters the Marketplace-assigned policy number from Form 1095-A, line 2.
Column b. Kara enters David's SSN.
Column c. Kara enters "01."
Column d. Kara enters "09."
Columns e, f, and g. Kara enters "0.10."
After completing Part 4, Kara completes her Form 8962 in the same manner described in Example 1 above.
David completes Worksheet C as follows.
David's Worksheet C. Allocations for Divorced or Legally Separated Taxpayer
1. Enter as a decimal your percentage from Step 1 above 1. .60
2. Enter 1.0 2. 1.0

3. Enter as a decimal the total of the percentages from Step 2 above allocated to the other taxpayer(s) 3. .45*
4. Subtract line 3 from line 2 4. .55

5. Multiply line 1 by line 4. Enter the result as a decimal. This is the allocation percentage. Go to Step 4 below 5. .33

*This is the total of David's agreed percentages with Lydia and Kimberly (.20 + .25).

After completing Worksheet C, David completes Form 8962, Part 4, line 30, as follows.

Column a. David enters the Marketplace-assigned policy number from Form 1095-A, line 2.

Column b. David enters Kara's SSN.

Column c. David enters "01."

Column d. David enters "09."

Columns e, f, and g. David enters "0.33."

After completing Part 4, David completes his Form 8962 in the same manner described in Example 1 above.

Lydia completes Worksheet D as follows.

Lydia's Worksheet D. Taxpayer Allocating with Divorced or Legally Separated Taxpayers

1. Enter the decimal from line 1 of the Worksheet C completed by the former spouse from Step 1 above 1. .40

2. Enter as a decimal the percentage from Step 1 above 2. .50

3. Multiply line 1 by line 2 3. .20

4. Enter the decimal from line 1 of the Worksheet C completed by the former spouse from Step 2 above 4. .60

5. Enter as a decimal the percentage from Step 2 above 5. .20

6. Multiply line 4 by line 5 6. .12

7. Add line 3 and line 6. This is the allocation percentage. Go to Step 4 below 7. .32

After completing Worksheet D, Lydia completes Form 8962, Part 4, line 30, as follows.

Column a. Lydia enters the Marketplace-assigned policy number from Form 1095-A, line 2.

Column b. Lydia enters Kara's SSN.

Column c. Lydia enters "01." Column d. Lydia enters "09."

Columns e, f, and g. Lydia enters "0.32."

After completing Part 4, Lydia completes her Form 8962 in the same manner as in Example 1 above.

Kimberly completes Worksheet D as follows.

Kimberly's Worksheet D. Taxpayer Allocating with Divorced or Legally Separated Taxpayers

1. Enter the decimal from line 1 of the Worksheet C completed by the former spouse from Step 1 above 1. .40
2. Enter as a decimal the percentage from Step 1 above 2. .25
3. Multiply line 1 by line 2 3. .10
4. Enter the decimal from line 1 of the Worksheet C completed by the former spouse from Step 2 above 4. .60
5. Enter as a decimal the percentage from Step 2 above 5. .25
6. Multiply line 4 by line 5 6. .15
7. Add line 3 and line 6. This is the allocation percentage. Go to Step 4 below 7. .25

After completing Worksheet D, Kimberly completes Form 8962, Part 4, line 30, as follows.

Column a. Kimberly enters the Marketplace-assigned policy number from Form 1095-A, line 2.

Column b. Kimberly enters Kara's SSN.

Column c. Kimberly enters "01."

Column d. Kimberly enters "09."

Columns e, f, and g. Kimberly enters "0.25."

After completing Part 4, Kimberly completes her Form 8962 in the same manner described for Lydia in Example 1 above.

Taxpayers Allocating Policy Amounts as Married But Not Filing a Joint Return and Because Individuals Enrolled With a Spouse's Tax Family Are Claimed by Another Taxpayer

Use this section if you meet either of the following conditions and no other allocations for the policy are necessary.

• You are allocating amounts with a spouse with whom you are legally married but not filing a joint return in 2014 and you also are allocating amounts with another taxpayer who is claiming a personal exemption for an individual who was enrolled in a qualified health plan with members of your and your spouse's tax families.

• You are the taxpayer who is claiming a personal exemption for an individual who was enrolled in the plan with tax family members of taxpayers who also must allocate policy amounts because the taxpayers are legally married but not filing a joint return in 2014.

Example. Pat and Jamie were married at the end of 2014 and have three dependent children, Jason, Alicia and Dawn. All five individuals enrolled in a qualified health plan and were covered for all of 2014. At enrollment, Pat and Jamie expected to file a joint return and claim personal exemptions for the children. However, Pat and Jamie change their minds and file as married filing separately and each claim only their own personal exemption. Neither checks the "Relief" box on Form 8962. Jason, Alicia, and Dawn moved in with their uncle, Andy, in April. Andy files as head of household and claims personal exemptions for Jason, Alicia, and Dawn.

Pat and Jamie use the allocation method under Married Taxpayers Allocating Because Not Filing a Joint Return and Also Allocating With Another Taxpayer .
Andy uses the allocation method under Taxpayer Allocating With Married Taxpayers Not Filing a Joint Return .
Married Taxpayers Allocating Because Not Filing a Joint Return and Also Allocating With Another Taxpayer

Use this allocation method if you are married but not filing a joint return and you must allocate policy amounts with your spouse and with a taxpayer claiming a personal exemption for an individual enrolled in a qualified health plan with members of your and your spouse's tax families. Under this method, you must first allocate 50% each of enrollment premiums and APTC to yourself and your spouse. Line 4 of Worksheet E, later, accomplishes this 50% allocation. Complete the steps below to determine the amounts to enter on your Form 8962, Part 4.

Step 1. Determine the applicable SLCSP for your coverage family. See Determining the Premium for the Applicable Second Lowest Cost Silver Plan (SLCSP) , earlier. For this purpose, your coverage family or your spouse's coverage family (but not both) should include the individual for whom the other taxpayer is claiming a personal exemption and who was enrolled in a qualified health plan with your and your spouse's tax family members. Enter the applicable SLCSP premium you determined on line 5 of Worksheet E.

Step 2. Separately from the first allocation, determine an allocation percentage with the taxpayer(s) claiming the personal exemption(s) for the individual(s) enrolled in the plan. You may agree on any allocation percentage between zero and one hundred percent. You may use the percentage you agreed on for every month in which this allocation rule applies, or you may agree on different percentages for different months. However, you must use the same allocation percentage for all policy amounts (enrollment premiums, applicable SLCSP premiums, and APTC) in a month. If you cannot agree on an allocation percentage, the allocation percentage is equal to the number of individuals for whom the other taxpayer claims a personal exemption for the tax year who were enrolled in the qualified health plan for which you are allocating amounts, divided by the total number of individuals enrolled in the plan. The allocation percentage is the percentage that applies to the amounts the taxpayer claiming the personal exemption must use to compute PTC and reconcile it with APTC. You must compute PTC and reconcile APTC using the remaining amounts.

Step 3. Complete Worksheet E below.
Worksheet E. Allocations for Married Taxpayers Not Filing a Joint Return
1. Enter 1.0 1. 1.0
2. Enter as a decimal the total of the percentage(s) from Step 2 above allocated to the other taxpayer(s) 2.
3. Subtract line 2 from line 1 3.
4. Divide line 3 by 2.0. Enter the result as a decimal 4.
5. Enter the applicable SLCSP premium as determined in Step 1 above 5.
6. Multiply line 5 by line 3. Complete Form 8962, Part 4, as instructed in Step 4 below 6.

Step 4. If you use the same percentage for every month during which this allocation method applies, use only one of lines 30-33 in Part 4 to report the allocation. If you use different percentages for different months under Step 2, use a separate line in Part 4 for each allocation percentage. Complete the line as explained below.

Column a. Enter the Marketplace-assigned policy number from Form 1095-A, line 2. If the policy number on the Form 1095-A is more than 15 characters, enter only the last 15 characters.
Column b. Enter the SSN of your spouse.
Column c. Enter the first month you are allocating policy amounts. For example, if you are allocating a percentage from January through June, enter "01" in column c.
Column d. Enter the last month you are allocating policy amounts. For example, if you are allocating a percentage from January through June, enter

"06" in column d.

Column e. If your filing status is married filing separately and you did not check the "Relief" box on the top right-hand corner of Form 8962, leave column e blank. If you checked the "Relief" box or Situation 1 under Married taxpayers in the instructions for Form 8962 applies to you, enter the decimal from line 4 of Worksheet E in column e.

Column f. If your filing status is married filing separately and you did not check the "Relief" box on the top right-hand corner of Form 8962, leave column f blank. If you checked the "Relief" box or Situation 1 under Married taxpayers in the instructions for Form 8962 applies to you, enter the decimal from line 3 of Worksheet E in column f and include the amount from line 6 of Worksheet E in the totals on the appropriate lines of Form 8962, column B, for the months allocated.

Column g. If APTC was paid, enter the decimal from line 4 of Worksheet E. If no APTC was paid, leave column g blank. If no APTC was paid, your filing status is married filing separately, and you did not check the "Relief" box on the top right-hand corner of Form 8962, stop. Do not file Form 8962 because you cannot take the PTC and you have no APTC to reconcile.

Taxpayer Allocating With Married Taxpayers Not Filing a Joint Return

Use this allocation method if you are claiming a personal exemption for an individual who was enrolled in a qualified health plan with tax family members of taxpayers who also must allocate policy amounts because the taxpayers are legally married but not filing a joint return in 2014.

Step 1. Determine an allocation percentage with one of the spouses. You may agree on any allocation percentage between zero and one hundred percent. You may use the percentage you agreed on for every month in which this allocation rule applies, or you may agree on different percentages for different months. However, you must use the same allocation percentage for all policy amounts (enrollment premiums, applicable SLCSP premiums, and APTC) in a month. If you cannot agree on an allocation percentage, the allocation percentage is equal to the number of individuals for whom you will claim a personal exemption for the tax year who were enrolled in the qualified health plan for which you are allocating policy amounts divided by the total number of individuals enrolled in the plan. The allocation percentage is the percentage that applies to the amounts you must use to compute PTC and reconcile it with APTC. The spouses must compute PTC and reconcile APTC using the remaining amounts. Enter the percentage as a decimal on line 1 of Worksheet F.

Step 2. Allocate the policy amounts with the second spouse using the same rules as Step 1 above. Enter the percentage as a decimal on line 3 of Worksheet F.

Step 3. Complete Worksheet F below.

Worksheet F. Taxpayer Allocating with Married Taxpayers Not Filing a Joint Return

Part I: Allocation Percentage for Enrollment Premiums and APTC Paid

1. Enter as a decimal the percentage from Step 1 above 1.

2. Divide line 1 by 2.0. Enter the result as a decimal 2.

3. Enter as a decimal the percentage from Step 2 above 3.

4. Divide line 3 by 2.0. Enter the result as a decimal 4.

5. Add lines 2 and 4. Enter the result as a decimal. This is your allocation percentage for enrollment premiums and APTC paid 5.

Part II: Allocation of the Applicable SLCSP Premium

Note. Complete this part only if APTC was paid. APTC is shown on Form 1095-A, Part III, column C.

6. Enter the amount of the applicable SLCSP premium from line 5 of Worksheet E completed by the spouse in Step 1 above 6.

7. Enter the decimal from line 1 of this worksheet 7.

8. Multiply line 6 by line 7 8.

9. Enter the amount of the applicable SLCSP premium from line 5 of Worksheet E completed by the spouse in Step 2 above 9.

10. Enter the decimal from line 3 of this worksheet 10.

11. Multiply line 9 by line 10 11.

12. Add lines 8 and 11. Enter the result as a decimal. This is the applicable SLCSP premium allocated to you that you must include on lines 12-23, column B, for the months in which this allocation applies 12.

Step 4. If you use the same percentage for every month during which this allocation method applies, use only one of lines 30-33 in Part 4 to report the allocation. If you use different percentages for different months, use a separate line in Part 4 for each allocation percentage. Complete the line as explained below.

Column a. Enter the Marketplace-assigned policy number from Form 1095-A, line 2. If the policy number on the Form 1095-A is more than 15 characters, enter only the last 15 characters.

Column b. Enter the SSN of the spouse whose percentage you entered in Worksheet F, line 1.

Column c. Enter the first month you are allocating policy amounts. For example, if you are allocating a percentage from January through June, enter "01" in column c.

Column d. Enter the last month you are allocating policy amounts. For example, if you are allocating a percentage from January through June, enter "06" in column c.

Column e. Enter the decimal from Worksheet F, line 5.

Column f. Leave column f blank.

Example. Pat and Jamie were married at the end of 2014 and have three dependent children, Jason, Alicia and Dawn. All five individuals enrolled in a qualified health plan and were covered for all of 2014. For each month of coverage, the enrollment premiums were $1,000, the premium for the applicable SLCSP for a coverage family of five was $800, and the APTC was $200. At enrollment, Pat and Jamie expected to file a joint return and claim personal exemptions for the children.

Jason, Alicia, and Dawn moved in with their uncle, Andy, in April. On their respective tax returns, Pat and Jamie file as married filing separately and each claim only their own personal exemption. Neither checks the "Relief" box on Form 8962. Andy files as head of household and claims personal exemptions for Jason, Alicia, and Dawn.

Pat and Jamie allocate the enrollment premiums and the APTC paid 50% to Pat and 50% to Jamie. Under Step 1 of Married Taxpayers Allocating Because Not Filing a Joint Return and Also Allocating With Another Taxpayer , Pat and Jamie determine that Pat's coverage family will include Pat, Jason, and Alicia and that Jamie's coverage family will include Jamie and Dawn. Pat and Jamie each look up their applicable SLCSP premiums. The applicable SLCSP premium for Pat's coverage family of three is $450 and the applicable SLCSP premium for Jamie's coverage family of two is $400.

Under Step 2 of that method (Pat, Jamie) and under the allocation method for Taxpayer Allocating With Married Taxpayers Not Filing a Joint Return. (Andy), Pat and Andy agree to allocate 67% of the policy amounts to Andy, and Jamie and Andy agree to allocate 50% of the policy amounts to Andy. Pat, Jamie, and Andy each complete a worksheet as shown below and use it to complete Part 4.

Pat completes Worksheet E as follows.
Pat's Worksheet E. Allocations for Married Taxpayers Not Filing a Joint Return
1. Enter 1.0 1. 1.0
2. Enter as a decimal the total of the percentage(s) from Step 2 above allocated to the other taxpayer(s) 2. 0.67
3. Subtract line 2 from line 1 3. 0.33
4. Divide line 3 by 2.0. Enter the result as a decimal 4. 0.17
5. Enter the applicable SLCSP premium as determined in Step 1 above 5. 450
6. Multiply line 5 by line 3. Complete Form 8962, Part 4, as instructed in Step 4 below 6. 149
After completing Worksheet E, Pat completes Form 8962, Part 4, line 30, as follows.
Column a. Pat enters the Marketplace-assigned policy number from Form 1095-A, line 2.
Column b. Pat enters Jamie's SSN.
Column c. Pat enters "01."
Column d. Pat enters "12."
Column e. Pat leaves this column blank.
Column f. Pat leaves this column blank. Column g. Pat enters "0.17."
After completing Part 4, Pat multiplies the APTC from Form 1095-A, Part III, column C, by the percentage in Part 4, column g, and enters $34 (APTC of $200 x 0.17) on Form 8962, lines 12-23, column F.
Jamie completes Worksheet E as follows.
Jamie's Worksheet E. Allocations for Married Taxpayers Not Filing a Joint Return
1. Enter 1.0 1. 1.0
2. Enter as a decimal the total of the percentage(s) from Step 2 above allocated to the other taxpayer(s).
Note. See Example 1 and Example 2 below for details on adding the percentages for multiple taxpayers 2. 0.50

3. Subtract line 2 from line 1 3. 0.50

4. Divide line 3 by 2.0. Enter the result as a decimal 4. 0.25

5. Enter the applicable SLCSP premium as determined in Step 1 above 5. 400

6. Multiply line 5 by line 3. Complete Form 8962, Part 4, as instructed in Step 4 below 6. 200

After completing Worksheet E, Jamie completes Form 8962, Part 4, line 30, as follows.

Column a. Jamie enters the Marketplace-assigned policy number from Form 1095-A, line 2.

Column b. Jamie enters Pat's SSN.

Column c. Jamie enters "01."

Column d. Jamie enters "12."

Column e. Jamie leaves this column blank.

Column f. Jamie leaves this column blank.

Column g. Jamie enters "0.25."

After completing Part 4, Jamie multiplies the APTC from Form 1095-A, Part III, column C, by the percentage in Part 4, column g, and enters $50 (APTC of $200 x 0.25) on Form 8962, lines 12-23, column F.

Andy completes Worksheet F as follows.

Andy's Worksheet F. Taxpayer Allocating with Married Taxpayers Not Filing a Joint Return Part I: Allocation Percentage for Enrollment Premiums and APTC Paid

1. Enter as a decimal the percentage from Step 1 above 1. 0.67

2. Divide line 1 by 2.0. Enter the result as a decimal 2. 0.34

3. Enter as a decimal the percentage from Step 2 above 3. 0.50

4. Divide line 3 by 2.0. Enter the result as a decimal 4. 0.25

5. Add lines 2 and 4. Enter the result as a decimal. This is your allocation percentage for enrollment premiums and APTC paid 5. 0.59

Part II: Allocation of the Applicable SLCSP Premium

Note. Complete this part only if APTC was paid. APTC is shown on Form 1095-A, Part III, column c.

6. Enter the amount of the applicable SLCSP premium from line 5 of Worksheet E completed by the spouse in Step 1 above 6. 450

7. Enter the decimal from line 1 of this worksheet 7. 0.67

8. Multiply line 6 by line 7 8. 302

9. Enter the amount of the applicable SLCSP premium from line 5 of

Worksheet E completed by the spouse in Step 2 above 9. 400
10. Enter the decimal from line 3 of this worksheet 10. 0.50
11. Multiply line 9 by line 10 11. 200
12. Add lines 8 and 11. Enter the result as a decimal. This is the applicable SLCSP premium allocated to you that you must include on lines 12-23, column B, for the months in which this allocation applies 12. 502
After completing Worksheet F, Andy completes Form 8962, Part 4, line 30, as follows.
Column a. Andy enters the Marketplace-assigned policy number from Form 1095-A, line 2.
Column b. Andy enters Pat's SSN.
Column c. Andy enters "01."
Column d. Andy enters "12."
Column e. Andy enters "0.59."
Column f. Andy leaves this column blank. Column g. Andy enters "0.59."

After completing Part 4, Andy multiplies the amounts from Form 1095-A, Part III, by the corresponding percentages in Part 4, and enters these allocated amounts on Form 8962, lines 12-23, columns A, B, and F. On each of those lines he will enter $590 in column A (enrollment premiums of $1,000 x 0.59), $502 in column B (applicable SLCSP premium allocated to him on Worksheet F, line 12), and $118 in column F (APTC of $200 x 0.59).

Taxpayers Allocating Policy Amounts for Individuals Claimed By Two or More Other Taxpayers

If you or another person in your tax family was enrolled in a qualified health plan with individuals in at least two other tax families, you and the taxpayers claiming the personal exemptions for the individuals not in your tax family should use the instructions for Form 8962 under Policy shared with an individual for whom another taxpayer claims a personal exemption to allocate amounts from the qualified health plan. There must be an allocation percentage for each taxpayer claiming a personal exemption for an individual who is enrolled in a qualified health plan with a member of your tax family. If you cannot agree on an allocation percentage with all taxpayers claiming personal exemptions for enrolled individuals, the allocation percentage for a particular taxpayer is equal to the number of individuals for whom the taxpayer will claim a personal exemption for the tax year who were enrolled in the qualified health plan for which you are allocating policy amounts, divided by the total number of individuals enrolled in the plan.

Example 1. Erik enrolled himself, his son, Bill, and his son, Arvind, in a qualified health plan with coverage effective for all of 2014. The enrollment premiums were $8,000, the premium for the applicable SLCSP for a coverage family consisting of Erik, Bill, and Arvind was $9,000, and the APTC paid for their coverage was $4,500. In March, Bill dropped out of school to work full-time and moved permanently into his own apartment. In May, Arvind moved in with his mother Sharon, where he lived until the end of 2014. On their respective tax returns, Erik files as single and claims his own personal exemption, Bill files as single and claims his own personal exemption, and Sharon files as head of household and claims a personal exemption for Arvind.

Erik and Bill agree to allocate 25% of the policy amounts to Bill. Erik and Sharon agree to allocate 40% of the policy amounts to Sharon. Erik allocates the remaining 35% of the policy amounts to himself.
Bill completes Form 8962, Part 4, line 30, as follows.
Column a. Bill enters the Marketplace-assigned policy number from Form 1095-A, line 2.
Column b. Bill enters Erik's SSN.
Column c. Bill enters "01."

Column d. Bill enters "12." Columns e, f, and g. Bill enters an allocation percentage of "0.25" in columns e, f, and g. (If no APTC was paid, he would not make an entry in columns f or g.)

After completing Part 4, Bill multiplies the amounts from Form 1095-A, Part III, by the corresponding percentages in Part 4, and enters these allocated amounts on his Form 8962, lines 12-23, columns A, B, and F. The sum of his monthly entries will be $2,000 in column A (enrollment premiums of $8,000 x 0.25), $2,250 in column B (applicable SLCSP premium of $9,000 x 0.25), and $1,125 in column F (APTC of $4,500 x 0.25).

Sharon completes Form 8962, Part 4, line 30, as follows.
Column a. Sharon enters the Marketplace-assigned policy number from Form 1095-A, line 2.
Column b. Sharon enters Erik's SSN.
Column c. Sharon enters "01."

Column d. Sharon enters "12."

Column e, f, and g. Sharon enters an allocation percentage of "0.40" in columns e, f, and g. (If no APTC was paid, she would not make any entry in columns f or g.)

After completing Part 4, Sharon multiplies the amounts from Form 1095-A, Part III, by the corresponding percentages in Part 4, and enters these allocated amounts on Form 8962, lines 12-23, columns A, B, and F. Her monthly entries will be $3,200 in column A (enrollment premiums of $8,000 x 0.40), $3,600 in column B (applicable SLCSP premium of $9,000 x 0.40), and $1,800 in column F (APTC of $4,500 x 0.40).

Erik completes Form 8962, Part 4, line 30, as follows.

Column a. Erik enters the Marketplace-assigned policy number from Form 1095-A, line 2.

Column b. Erik enters either Bill's SSN or Sharon's SSN.

Column c. Erik enters "01."

Column d. Erik enters "12."

Column e, f, and g. Erik enters an allocation percentage of "0.35" in columns e, f, and g, which is the percentage of policy amounts not allocated to Bill or Sharon. (If no APTC was paid, he would not make any entry in columns f or g.)

After completing Part 4, Erik multiplies the amounts from Form 1095-A, Part III, by the corresponding percentages in Part 4, and enters these allocated amounts on his Form 8962, lines 12-23, columns A, B, and F. The sum of his monthly entries will be $2,800 in column A (enrollment premiums of $8,000 x 0.35), $3,150 in column B (applicable SLCSP of $9,000 x 0.35), and $1,575 in column F (APTC of $4,500 x 0.35).

Example 2. The facts are the same as Example 1 except Erik and Bill cannot agree on an allocation percentage. Because Erik did not agree on an allocation percentage with all taxpayers claiming personal exemptions for individuals not in his tax family, Bill and Sharon determine their allocation percentages of 33% by dividing the number of enrolled individuals for whom each will claim a personal exemption (1 each for Bill and Sharon) by the number of individuals enrolled in the plan (3, Erik, Bill, and Arvind). Erik's allocation percentage is 34%, which is the percentage of policy amounts not allocated to Bill and Sharon. Each taxpayer completes Part 4 as explained in

Example 1 using these percentages.

## Alternative Calculation for Year of Marriage

Before you read this section, first read the instructions for line 9 in the instructions for Form 8962. Complete Table 4 and, if required, Worksheet 2 in those instructions. Then continue reading this section if you meet either of the following conditions.

• You checked the "No" box on Form 8962, line 6, and you answered "Yes" to all 5 questions in Table 4.
• You checked the "Yes" boxes on Form 8962, line 6, and on line 14 of Worksheet 2.
If you do not meet either of the above conditions, you are not eligible to elect the alternative calculation. Leave Form 8962, Part 5, blank.

If you are eligible, electing the alternative calculation may reduce the amount of excess APTC you have to repay. Electing the alternative calculation is optional. Worksheet V (shown later) will tell you whether the alternative calculation will benefit you.

You must complete a worksheet only if you are enrolled in coverage or you enrolled another individual in your tax family in coverage. Your spouse must complete a worksheet only if your spouse enrolled in coverage or enrolled another individual in your tax family in coverage.

## Which Steps To Complete

• Only if you were enrolled in coverage under a qualified health plan, or if you enrolled an individual in your tax family in coverage, for one or more of your pre-marriage months, complete Steps 1, 2, and 5.

• Only if your spouse was enrolled in coverage under a qualified health plan, or enrolled an individual in your tax family in coverage, for one or more of your pre-marriage months, complete Steps 3, 4, and 5.

• If an individual in your tax family was enrolled in coverage under a qualified health plan, but not by either you or your spouse for any of your pre-marriage months, you may include that individual in either Steps 1, 2, and 5 if you enrolled someone or Steps 3, 4, and 5 if your spouse enrolled someone.

• The instructions for Step 5 will prompt you to complete Worksheet V. If you check the "Yes" box on Worksheet V, line 14, complete Steps 6, 7, and 8.

Your pre-marriage months include the month you got married.
Before you begin the steps, determine your alternative family size and your spouse's alternative family size using the instructions under Alternative family size , later.
If you completed Part 4 of Form 8962, do not include any amounts from Form(s) 1095-A that were allocated to another taxpayer when completing the steps for your alternative calculation.

Alternative family size. Your alternative family size is used to determine an alternative monthly contribution amount (see Monthly contribution amount under Terms You May Need to Know in the Instructions for Form 8962) on Worksheets I and III, which may reduce the amount of excess APTC for the pre-marriage months that you must repay. When determining your alternative family size, include yourself and any individual in the tax family who qualifies as your dependent for the year under the rules explained in the instructions for Form 1040 or 1040A, line 6c, or Form 1040NR, line 7c. Do not include any individual who does not qualify as your dependent under those rules or who is included in your spouse's alternative family size.

When determining your spouse's alternative family size, include your spouse and any individual in the tax family who qualifies as your spouse's dependent for the year under the rules explained in the instructions for Form 1040 or 1040A, line 6c, or Form 1040NR, line 7c. Do not include any individual who does not qualify as your spouse's dependent under those rules or who is included in your alternative family size.

Note.
You may include an individual who qualifies as the dependent of both you and your spouse in either alternative family size.

Example 1. Ron, Suzy, and their son Max have lived together since July 2013. Ron and Suzy got married in August 2014. Each of them had coverage under a qualified health plan for the months before September. Max qualifies as Ron's dependent under the rules explained in the instructions for Form 1040, line 6c. Max also qualifies as Suzy's dependent under those rules. Ron and Suzy can include Max in either alternative family size.

Example 2. Rob and his son Liam lived together from January through May 2014. On June 10, 2014, Rob married Tara. She moved in with Rob and Liam on June 11. Each of them had coverage under a qualified health plan for the months before July. Liam qualifies as Rob's dependent under the rules explained in the instructions for Form 1040, line 6c. Liam also qualifies as Tara's dependent under those rules. (Liam is Tara's stepchild and lived with Tara for more than half of 2014.) Rob and Tara can include Liam in either alternative family size.

Example 3. Stacey and her daughter Leia lived together from January through July 2014. Stacey married Vince in August 2014 and Vince moved in with Stacey and Leia. Each of them had coverage under a qualified health plan for the months before September. Leia qualifies as Stacey's dependent under the rules explained in the instructions for Form 1040, line 6c. Leia does not qualify as Vince's dependent under those rules because Leia did not live with Vince for more than half of 2014. Stacey must include Leia in her alternative family size. Vince cannot include Leia in his alternative family size.

Step 1.

Complete Worksheet I, later, if you meet the condition described in the first bullet below. Also complete Worksheet I for an individual described in the second bullet.

• You were enrolled in coverage under a qualified health plan, or you enrolled an individual included in your tax family in coverage, for one or more of your pre-marriage months.

• An individual in your tax family was enrolled in coverage under a qualified health plan, but not by either you or your spouse for any of your pre-marriage months, you enrolled someone in a qualified health plan, and you include that individual in Steps 1, 2, and 5.

Step 2.

Complete Worksheet II, later, to determine your alternative monthly credit amounts to include on Form 8962, lines 12–23, column E, for your pre-marriage months. Enter in columns A and B on Worksheet II the amounts from columns A and B in Part III of the Form(s) 1095-A that reports coverage for the individuals for whom you completed Step 1.

Note.

For your pre-marriage months, if there were changes in your coverage family that you did not report to the Marketplace or APTC was not paid for the coverage, you may have to determine a new premium for your applicable SLCSP for those months. See Determining the Premium for the Applicable Second Lowest Cost Silver Plan (SLCSP) , earlier.

Step 3.
Complete Worksheet III, later, if your spouse meets the condition described in the first bullet below. Also complete Worksheet III for an individual described in the second bullet.
• Your spouse was enrolled in coverage under a qualified health plan, or your spouse enrolled an individual included in your tax family in coverage, for one or more of your pre-marriage months.

• An individual in your tax family was enrolled in coverage under a qualified health plan, but not by either you or your spouse for any of your pre-marriage months, your spouse enrolled someone in a qualified health plan, and your spouse includes that individual in Steps 3, 4, and 5.

Step 4. Complete Worksheet IV, later, to determine your spouse's alternative monthly credit amounts to include on Form 8962, lines 12–23, column E, for your pre-marriage months. Enter in columns A and B on Worksheet IV the amounts from columns A and B in Part III of the Form(s) 1095-A that reports coverage for the individuals for whom you completed Step 3.

Note.

For your pre-marriage months, if there were changes in your spouse's coverage family that your spouse did not report to the Marketplace or APTC was not paid for the coverage, your spouse may have to determine a new premium for the applicable SLCSP for those months. See Determining the Premium for the Applicable Second Lowest Cost Silver Plan (SLCSP) , earlier.

Step 5.
After you have completed Steps 1 and 2 and/or Steps 3 and 4, complete Worksheet V, later, to determine what entries you must make on Form 8962, lines 12–23, for your pre-marriage months.

Step 6.
Complete Form 8962, lines 35 and 36 using the following instructions.
Follow these instructions only if you checked the "Yes" box on Worksheet V, line 14.
Line 35.
• Column a: Enter the family size from Worksheet I, line 1.
• Column b: Enter the amount from Worksheet I, line 7.
• Column c: Enter the month from Worksheet I, line 8.
• Column d: Enter the month from Worksheet I, line 9.
Line 36.
• Column a: Enter the family size from Worksheet III, line 1.
• Column b: Enter the amount from Worksheet III, line 7.
• Column c: Enter the month from Worksheet III, line 8.
• Column d: Enter the month from Worksheet III, line 9.
Step 7.
Complete Form 8962, lines 12–23, columns A–F, using the following instructions. Follow these instructions only if you checked the "Yes" box on Worksheet V, line 14.
Column A. Enter the amounts from column A of Worksheet 2 in the Form 8962 instructions. Column B. Enter the amounts from column B of Worksheet 2 in the Form 8962 instructions.

Column C. For pre-marriage months, enter the totals of Worksheet II, column C, and Worksheet IV, column C. For example, if you entered $200 on Worksheet II, column C, lines 1–5, and you entered $250 on Worksheet IV, column C, lines 3–5, enter $200 on lines 12 and 13, and $450 on lines 14–16 of Form 8962, column C.

For the months you were married for the entire month, enter the amount from Form 8962, line 8b.
Column D. Subtract column C from column B and enter the result. If zero or less, enter zero.
Column E. For your pre-marriage months, enter the amounts from lines 1–12, column A, of Worksheet V, later, in the boxes for the corresponding months in column E.
For the months you were married for the entire month, enter the smaller of column A or D.
Column F. Enter the amounts from column F of Worksheet 2 in the Form

8962 instructions.

Step 8.

Continue to Form 8962, line 24, and complete the rest of the form.

Worksheet I. Your Alternative Monthly Contribution Amount

1. Alternative family size: Enter the total number of individuals in your alternative family size (discussed earlier) 1.

2. One-half of household income: Divide Form 8962, line 3, by 2. Round to the nearest whole dollar amount2.

3. Alternative Federal poverty line: Enter the Federal poverty amount as determined by your alternative family size on line 1 above and the Federal poverty table you used on Form 8962, line 4 3.

4. Alternative household income as a percentage of Federal poverty line: Divide line 2 by line 3. Enter the result rounded to a whole percentage. Use the same rounding rules provided under Line 5 of the Instructions for Form 8962. If the result is more than 400, stop. Do not complete the rest of this worksheet or Step 2. Continue to Step 3 if you were instructed to complete that step by the second or third bullet under Which Steps To Complete , earlier. Otherwise, if you did not complete Part 4 of Form 8962, check the "No" box on line 9 of Form 8962 and continue to line 10. If you completed Part 4 of Form 8962, check the "No" box on line 10, and see Lines 12 through 23—Monthly Calculation in the Instructions for Form 8962 4.

5. Alternative applicable figure: Using your line 4 percentage, locate your applicable figure on Table 2 in the Instructions for Form 8962 5.

6. Multiply line 2 by line 5 6.

7. Alternative monthly contribution for health care: Divide line 6 by 12 and enter the result rounded to the nearest whole dollar amount 7.

8. Alternative start month: Enter the first full month you or any individual included in your alternative family size on line 1 had coverage under a qualified health plan. For example, enter "02" if you were enrolled in a qualified health plan with coverage effective on February 1 8.

9. Alternative stop month: Enter the last month you or any individual included in your alternative family size on line 1 had coverage under a qualified health plan or the month in which you got married, whichever is earlier. For example, enter "09" if you had coverage under a qualified health

plan for all of 2014 and you got married on September 5 9.

Worksheet II. Your Alternative Monthly Credit Amounts for Pre-Marriage Months

Complete this worksheet only for months beginning with the month on line 8 of Worksheet I and ending with the month on line 9 of Worksheet I. For example, if you entered "02" on Worksheet I, line 8, and "10" on Worksheet I, line 9, complete only lines 2–10 of this worksheet.

Monthly Calculation A. Form(s) 1095-A, lines 21–32, column A* B. Form(s) 1095-A, lines 21–32, column B* C. Worksheet I, line 7 D. Subtract column C from column B** E. Smaller of column A or column D

1 January
2 February
3 March
4 April
5 May
6 June
7 July
8 August
9 September
10 October
11 November
12 December
*See Step 2 , earlier, for instructions on the Form 1095-A amounts to report on this worksheet. **If zero or less, enter -0-.
After completing this worksheet: Continue to Step 3 if you were instructed to complete that step by the second or third bullet under Which Steps To Complete , earlier. Otherwise, go to Step 5 .
Worksheet III. Your Spouse's Alternative Monthly Contribution Amount
1. Alternative family size: Enter the total number of individuals in your spouse's alternative family size (discussed earlier) 1.
2. One-half of household income: Divide Form 8962, line 3, by 2. Round to the nearest whole dollar amount2.

3. Alternative Federal poverty line: Enter the Federal poverty amount as determined by your spouse's alternative family size on line 1 above and the

Federal poverty table you used on Form 8962, line 4 3.

4. Alternative household income as a percentage of Federal poverty line: Divide line 2 by line 3. Enter the result rounded to a whole percentage. Use the same rounding rules provided under Line 5 of the Instructions for Form 8962. If the result is more than 400, stop. Do not complete the rest of this worksheet or Step 4. If you completed Step 2, continue to Step 5. If you did not complete Step 2 and you did not complete Part 4 of Form 8962, check the "No" box on line 9 of Form 8962 and continue to line 10. If you did not complete Step 2 and you completed Part 4 of Form 8962, check the "No" box on line 10, and see Lines 12 through 23—Monthly Calculation in the Instructions for Form 8962 4.

5. Alternative applicable figure: Using your line 4 percentage, locate your applicable figure on Table 2 in the Instructions for Form 8962 5.
6. Multiply line 2 by line 5 6.
7. Alternative monthly contribution for health care: Divide line 6 by 12 and enter the result rounded to the nearest whole dollar amount 7.

8. Alternative start month: Enter the first full month your spouse or any individual included in your spouse's alternative family size on line 1 had coverage under a qualified health plan. For example, enter "05" if your spouse was enrolled in a qualified health plan with coverage effective on May 1 . . . 8.

9. Alternative stop month: Enter the last month your spouse or any individual included in your spouse's alternative family size on line 1 had coverage under a qualified health plan or the month in which you got married, whichever is earlier. For example, enter "07" if your spouse's coverage under a qualified health plan (and the coverage of all individuals included in your spouse's alternative family size) terminated July 31 and you got married on September 5 9.

Worksheet IV. Your Spouse's Alternative Monthly Credit Amounts for Pre-Marriage Months

Complete this worksheet only for months beginning with the month on line 8 of Worksheet III and ending with the month on line 9 of Worksheet III. For example, if you entered "05" on Worksheet III, line 8, and "10" on Worksheet III, line 9, complete only lines 5–10 of this worksheet.

Monthly Calculation A. Form(s) 1095-A, lines 21–32, column A* B. Form(s) 1095-A, lines 21–32, column B* C. Worksheet III, line 7 D. Subtract column C from column B** E. Smaller of column A or column D

1 January
2 February
3 March
4 April
5 May
6 June
7 July
8 August
9 September
10 October
11 November
12 December

*See Step 4 , earlier, for instructions on the Form 1095-A amounts to report on this worksheet.

**If zero or less, enter -0-.

After completing this worksheet: Continue to Step 5 .

Worksheet V. Alternative Calculation for Year of Marriage Totals Worksheet

Column A. Complete column A below only for the months you have entries in column E of Worksheet II and/or Worksheet IV. Leave column A blank for all other months. Add the amounts in column E of Worksheets II and IV separately for each month and enter the total in column A below on the line for the same month.

Column B. Complete column B below for any month you have an entry in column A. For each month, enter the corresponding amount from lines 1–12, column E, of Worksheet 2 under Line 9 in the Instructions for Form 8962. If you did not complete Worksheet 2 because you entered more than 400 on Form 8962, line 5, leave column B, lines 1–12, blank and enter -0- on line 13.

Monthly Calculation A. Total Alternative Premium Assistance Amounts B. Premium Assistance Amounts (Regular Calculation)

1 January 1
2 February 2
3 March 3
4 April 4

5 May 5
6 June 6
7 July 7
8 August 8
9 September 9
10 October 10
11 November 11
12 December 12
13 Totals: Enter the total of column A, lines 1–12, and the total of column B, lines 1–12 13
14 Is line 13, column A, more than line 13, column B?

❏ Yes. Your alternative calculation reduces your excess APTC. If you did not complete Part 4 of Form 8962, check the "Yes" box on line 9. Continue to Steps 6, 7, and 8, earlier.

❏ No. The alternative calculation does not reduce your excess APTC. Leave Form 8962, Part 5, blank.

• If you did not complete Part 4 of Form 8962, check the "No" box on line 9 and continue to Form 8962, line 10. If you are required to use lines 12 through 23 of Form 8962, enter the amounts from lines 1 through 12 of Worksheet 2 in the Form 8962 instructions on the lines for the corresponding months and columns on Form 8962.

• If you completed Part 4 of Form 8962, check the "No" box on line 10. Enter the amounts from lines 1 through 12 of Worksheet 2 in the Form 8962 instructions on the lines for the corresponding months and columns on Form 8962, lines 12 through 23.

Self-Employed Health Insurance Deduction and PTC

This part provides special instructions for figuring the self-employed health insurance deduction and PTC if you or your spouse was self-employed, you or a member of your tax family was enrolled in a qualified health plan in 2014, and you are eligible for the PTC. Because the amount of the self-employed health insurance deduction is based on the amount of the PTC and the amount of the PTC is based on the amount of the deduction, a taxpayer who may be eligible for both may have difficulty determining the amounts of those items. A taxpayer who may be eligible for both may follow the instructions in this part to determine amounts of the self-employed health insurance deduction and PTC that follow the law.

Using the instructions in this part is optional. If you are eligible for both a self-employed health insurance deduction and PTC for the same premiums, you may use any computation method that satisfies each set of rules as long as the sum of the deduction claimed for the premiums and the PTC computed, taking the deduction into account, is less than or equal to the premiums.

Before you complete any of the worksheets in this part, you should first do the following.
• Read the instructions for line 29 of Form 1040 or Form 1040NR to find out if you meet the requirements for claiming the self-employed health insurance deduction.

• Read the Instructions for Form 8962 to find out if you meet the requirements for claiming the PTC except for the requirement that your household income be at least 100% but not more than 400% of the Federal poverty line for your family size for 2014. You will determine whether you meet the 100%
– 400% requirement in the process of completing these instructions.

If you meet the requirements described above, do the following.
• If you are filing Form 1040, complete lines 30 and 31a. Also, figure any write-in adjustments you will enter on the dotted line next to line 36.
• If you are filing Form 1040NR, complete lines 30 and 31a. Also, figure any write-in adjustments you will enter on the dotted line next to line 35.
• If you elect to report your child's interest and dividends on your tax return, complete Form 8814.

Using this information, do the following. 1. If you have health insurance premiums for which you cannot claim the PTC (see Nonspecified premiums , later), first complete Worksheet P, or if required, Worksheet 6-A in chapter 6 of . 535 but only with respect to those premiums. Skip Worksheets W and X if either of the following applies.

a. You completed Worksheet P and line 3 is less than line 1.
b. You completed Worksheet 6-A in chapter 6 of . 535 and line 13 is equal to or less than line 3.

2. Then complete Worksheet W and Worksheet X. Note that you only have to

complete Worksheet W if advance payments of the premium tax credit (APTC) were made to your insurer on your behalf for the months you were self-employed. If APTC was not paid to your insurer on your behalf for the months you were self-employed, skip Worksheet W.

3. After completing Worksheets W and X, you may choose to use either the Simplified Calculation Method or the Iterative Calculation Method to compute your self-employed health insurance deduction and PTC. The Simplified Calculation Method is shorter, but in some cases will not produce a result as favorable as the Iterative Calculation Method.

Worksheet P. Self-Employed Health Insurance Deduction for Nonspecified Premiums

Before you begin: ✓ Read Exceptions , later, to see if you can use this worksheet instead of . 535 to figure your deduction for nonspecified premiums. Also read the definitions of specified premiums and nonspecified premiums, later.

1. Enter the total amount of nonspecified premiums paid in 2014 for health insurance coverage established under your business (or the S corporation in which you were a more-than-2% shareholder) for 2014 for you, your spouse, and your dependents. Your insurance can also cover your child who was under age 27 at the end of 2014, even if the child was not your dependent. But do not include amounts for any month you were eligible to participate in an employer-sponsored health plan or amounts paid from retirement plan distributions that were nontaxable because you are a retired public safety officer 1.

2. Enter your net profit* and any other earned income** from the business under which the insurance plan is established, minus any deductions on lines 27 and 28 of Form 1040 or 1040NR. Do not include Conservation Reserve Program payments exempt from self-employment tax 2.

3. Self-employed health insurance deduction for nonspecified premiums. Enter the smaller of line 1 or line 2. Do not include this amount in figuring any medical expense deduction on Schedule A (Form 1040) 3.

• If line 2 is equal to or less than line 1, stop here. Do not read the rest of these special instructions. Enter this amount on line 29 of Form 1040 or

1040NR. Use Form 8962 to figure the premium tax credit for specified premiums.

• If line 2 is more than line 1, complete Worksheet W if APTC was paid to your insurer on your

behalf for the months you were self-employed. If APTC was not paid to your insurer on your behalf for the months you were self-employed, skip Worksheet W and go to Worksheet X.

*If you used either optional method to figure your net earnings from self-employment, do not enter your net profit. Instead, enter the amount from Schedule SE, Section B, line 4b.

**Earned incomeincludes net earnings and gains from the sale, transfer, or licensing of property you created. However, it does not include capital gain income. If you were a more-than-2% shareholder in the S corporation under which the insurance plan is established, earned income is your Medicare wages (box 5 of Form W-2) from that corporation.

Instructions for Worksheet P
Use Worksheet P, earlier, to figure the amount you can deduct for nonspecified premiums.

Exceptions. Use Worksheet 6-A in chapter 6 of . 535 instead of Worksheet P to figure your deduction for nonspecified premiums if any of the following applies. (Only include nonspecified premiums on line 1 or 2 of Worksheet 6-A.)

• You had more than one source of income subject to self-employment tax.
• You file Form 2555 or 2555-EZ.
• You are using amounts paid for qualified long-term care insurance to figure the deduction.
After you complete Worksheet 6-A, follow the instructions below.

• If line 13 is equal to or less than line 3, stop here. Do not read the rest of these special instructions. Enter the amount from line 14 of Worksheet 6-A on line 29 of Form 1040 or 1040NR. Use Form 8962 to figure the premium tax credit for specified premiums.

• If line 13 is more than line 3, complete Worksheet W if APTC was paid to your insurer on your behalf for the months you were self-employed. If APTC was not paid to your insurer on your behalf for the months you were self-employed, skip Worksheet W and go to Worksheet X.

Nonspecified premiums. A nonspecified premium is either of the following.
• A premium for health insurance coverage established under your business (or the S corporation in which you were a more-than-2%-shareholder) but paid for coverage in a plan that is not a qualified health plan.

• The portion of the premium for coverage in a plan that is a qualified health plan established under your business (or the S corporation in which you were a more-than-2%-shareholder) but that is attributable to individuals not in your coverage family.

Calculate how much of these nonspecified premiums are fully deductible by entering this amount on line 1 of Worksheet P, or if required, on line 1 or 2 of Worksheet 6-A in chapter 6 of . 535. Complete the remainder of the appropriate worksheet.

The following are examples of nonspecified premiums.
• Premiums paid for a qualified health plan other than during a coverage month.
• Premiums paid to cover an individual other than you, your spouse, or your dependents.
• Premiums for qualified long-term care insurance.
• Dental insurance premiums.
• Medicare premiums you voluntarily paid to obtain insurance in your name that is similar to qualifying health insurance.

Example. In 2014, you were self-employed and were enrolled in a qualified health plan through the Marketplace. You enrolled your dependent, 22-year old daughter in individual market coverage not offered through the Marketplace. This coverage has an annual premium of $3,000. This $3,000 premium is a nonspecified premium because it is for coverage under a plan that is not a qualified health plan. Include this $3,000 premium on Worksheet P, line 1, or if required, on line 1 of the Worksheet 6-A in chapter 6 of . 535.

Specified premiums. Specified premiums are the premiums for a specified qualified health plan or plans for which you may otherwise claim as a self-employed health insurance deduction on line 29 of Form 1040 or Form 1040NR. Generally, these are the premiums paid for the months you were self-employed. If you were self-employed for part of a month, the entire premium for that month is a specified premium. A specified qualified health plan is a qualified health plan that covers one or more members of your coverage family for a month for which your enrollment premium(s) have been paid by the due date of your tax return (not including extensions). Qualified health plan, coverage family, and enrollment premiums are defined in the Form 8962 instructions.

If the plan covers individuals who are not in your coverage family, use only the portion of the premiums for the specified qualified health plan that is allocable to your coverage family. You determine the specified premiums that are allocable to your coverage family by multiplying the enrollment premiums for the months you were self-employed and the plan covered non-coverage family members by a fraction. The numerator of the fraction is the premium for the applicable second lowest cost silver plan (SLCSP) for your coverage family. The denominator of the fraction is the total of (1) the premium for the applicable SLCSP for your coverage family and (2) the premium for the applicable SLCSP for the individuals who are not in your coverage family. See Example 2 below.

Example 1. You were enrolled in a qualified health plan through the Marketplace for all of 2014 and you were self-employed from September 15 through December 31. Only the premiums for the last 4 months are specified premiums and only those premiums are entered on Worksheet W, line 5, and Worksheet X, line 1, if you are required to complete those worksheets. You are not allowed a selfemployed health insurance deduction for the January – August premiums because you were not selfemployed during those months. Those premiums are neither specified premiums nor nonspecified premiums. However, you may be allowed a PTC for your coverage for January – August.

Example 2. Gary was self-employed in 2014 and enrolled in a qualified health plan. APTC was paid to his insurer on his behalf. The policy covers Gary, Gary's two dependent daughters, and Gary's 25-year old nondependent son Jim. The enrollment premium is $15,000. The premium for the applicable SLCSP covering Gary and his two daughters is $12,000 and the premium for the applicable SLCSP covering Jim is $6,000. Gary figures the amount of specified premiums by multiplying the $15,000 enrollment premium by a fraction. The numerator of the fraction is the premium for his applicable

SLCSP ($12,000). The denominator of the fraction is the total of the premiums for the applicable SLCSP of both Gary and Jim ($18,000). The result is $10,000 ($15,000 enrollment premium x ($12,000/$18,000)) of specified premiums, which Gary enters on Worksheet W, line 5, and Worksheet X, line 1. The remaining $5,000 of enrollment premium ($15,000 enrollment premium - $10,000 specified premiums) is attributable to Jim's coverage and is a nonspecified premium that Gary enters on Worksheet P, line 1.

Worksheet W. Figuring Household Income and the Limitation on Additional Tax
Part I: Taxpayer's Modified AGI
1. Combine the amounts from:
• Form 1040, lines 8b, 22, and the excess, if any, of line 20a over line 20b.
• Form 1040NR, lines 9b and 23 1.
Note. See instructions if you are filing Form 8582, 8814, or 8815.
2. Enter any amounts from Form 2555, lines 45 and 50, and Form 2555-EZ, line 18 2.
3. Add lines 1 and 2 3.
4a. Enter the total of the amounts from:

• Form 1040, lines 23 through 28, 30, and 31a, plus any write-in adjustments you entered on the dotted line next to line 36.
• Form 1040NR, lines 24 through 28, 30, and 31, plus any write-in adjustments you entered on the dotted line next to line 35 4a.

4b. Enter your self-employed health insurance deduction for nonspecified premiums from Worksheet P, line 3, or Worksheet 6-A, line 14, in chapter 6 of . 535 4b.
5. Enter specified premiums (see Specified premiums under Instructions for Worksheet P, earlier)
5.
6. Enter APTC attributable to the premiums on line 5 (see instructions) 6.
7. Subtract line 6 from line 5 7.
8. Add lines 4a, 4b, and 7 8.
9. Subtract line 8 from line 3. Then go to Part II if you are claiming dependents on your tax return. If you are not claiming any dependents on your tax return, skip Part II and go to Part III 9.
Part II: Dependents' Modified AGI

Note. Use Part II to figure the combined modified AGI for the dependents you claimed as exemptions on your return. Only include the modified AGI of those dependents who are required to file a return. Do not include the modified AGI of dependents who are filing a tax return only to claim a refund of tax withheld or estimated tax.

10. Enter the combined AGI for your dependents from Form 1040, line 38; Form 1040A, line 22; Form 1040EZ, line 4; and Form 1040NR, line 37 10.

11. Enter any tax-exempt interest for your dependents from Form 1040, line 8b; Form 1040A, line 8b; Form 1040EZ, the amount written to the left of the line 2 entry space; and Form 1040NR, line 9b 11.

12. Enter any amounts for your dependents from Form 2555, lines 45 and 50, and Form 2555-EZ, line 18 12.

13. Enter for each of your dependents the excess, if any, of Form 1040, line 20a over line 20b; and Form 1040A, line 14a over line 14b 13.

14. Add lines 10 through 13. Then go to Part III 14.

Continued on next page. Worksheet W. Figuring Household Income and the Limitation on Additional Tax (continued)

Part III: Limitation on Additional Tax

15. Household income. Add lines 9 and 14 15.

16. Enter $600 ($300 if your filing status is single) 16.

17. 17. 17.

18a. Enter the number of exemptions from Form 1040, line 6d, or Form 1040NR, line 7d 18a.

18b. Enter the Federal poverty amount as determined by the family size on line 18a and Federal poverty Table 1-1, 1-2, or 1-3 for your state of residence during 2014 in the Form 8962 instructions 18b.

19. Divide line 17 by line 18b. Enter the result rounded to a whole percentage. For example, enter
154 if the percentage is 1.542 and enter 155 if the percentage is 1.549. See the instructions for lines 19,
22, and 25 for special rules 19.

• If the result is less than 200, enter the amount from line 16 on line 26. Skip lines 20–25.
• If the result is 200 or more, go to line 20.

20. Enter $1,500 ($750 if your filing status is single) 20.

21. 21. 21.

22. Divide line 21 by line 18b. Enter the result rounded to a whole percentage. For example, enter
154 if the percentage is 1.542 and enter 155 if the percentage is 1.549. See the instructions for lines 19,
22, and 25 for special rules 22.

• If the result is less than 300, enter the amount from line 20 on line 26. Skip lines 23–25.
• If the result is 300 or more, go to line 23.
23. Enter $2,500 ($1,250 if your filing status is single) 23.
24. 24. 24.

25. Divide line 24 by line 18b. Enter the result rounded to a whole percentage. For example, enter
154 if the percentage is 1.542 and enter 155 if the percentage is 1.549. See the instructions for lines 19,
22, and 25 for special rules 25.

• If the result is less than 400, enter the amount from line 23 on line 26.
• If the result is 400 or more, enter the amount from line 6 on line 26. 26. Enter the amount you were instructed to enter here by line 19, 22, or 25 26.
27. Add lines 7 and 26. 27.
28. Enter the smaller of line 5 or line 27. Then go to Worksheet X.
28.

Instructions for Worksheet W
Line 1. If you are filing Form 8582, Passive Activity Loss Limitations, and both lines 1d and 4 of that form are losses:
• Do not complete Parts II, III, or IV of that form until you are instructed to do so later, and
• Do not include any losses from rental real estate activities on line 1.
If you are filing Form 8814, Parents' Election to Report Child's Interest and Dividends, and the amount on Form 8814, line 4, is more than $1,000, you must also include the following amounts on line 1.
• The tax-exempt interest from Form 8814, line 1b.
• The lesser of Form 8814, line 4 or line 5.
• Any nontaxable social security benefits your child received.

If you are filing Form 8815, Exclusion of Interest From Series EE and I U.S. Savings Bonds Issued After 1989, do not complete the form until you are instructed to do so later. Include on line 1 the amount from Schedule B (Form 1040A or 1040), line 2.

Line 6. Enter on this line the APTC from Form 1095-A, Part III, column C, that is attributable to specified premiums on line 5.

Lines 19, 22, and 25. If the result is between 1.00 and 3.99, round up or down to the nearest whole percentage. For example, for 1.854, enter the result as 185; for 3.565, enter the result as 357.

If the result is less than 1.00 or more than 3.99, round the result as follows.

• For any amount less than 1.00, round down to the nearest whole percentage. For example, for .996, enter the result as 99.

• For any amount between 3.99 and 4.00, round down to 399. For example, for 3.998, enter the result as 399.

• For any amount more than 4.00 but less than 9.99, round up to the nearest whole percentage. For example, for 4.004, enter the result as 401.

• For an amount more than 9.99, enter the result as 999. For example, for 10.456, enter the result as 999.

Worksheet X. Figuring the Limit Under Section 5.03 of Revenue Procedure 2014-41

Note. If you have more than one trade or business under which a qualified health plan is established, complete lines 2-11 separately for each trade or business. Add the amounts on line 11 for all the trades or businesses. Then complete lines 12-15 once for all trades or businesses.

1. Enter the amount from Worksheet W, line 28. If you did not complete Worksheet W, enter your specified premiums. See Specified premiums under Instructions for Worksheet P, earlier.
1.

2. Enter your net profit* and any other earned income** from the business under which the qualified health plan is established. Do not include Conservation Reserve Program payments exempt from self-employment tax. If the business is an S corporation, skip to line 9 2.

3. Enter the total of all net profits* from: Schedule C (Form 1040), line 31;

Schedule C-EZ (Form
1040), line 3; Schedule F (Form 1040), line 34; or Schedule K-1 (Form
1065), box 14, code A; plus any other income allocable to the profitable
businesses. Do not include Conservation Reserve Program payments exempt
from self-employment tax. See the Instructions for Schedule SE (Form 1040).
Do not include any net losses shown on these schedules 3.

4. Divide line 2 by line 3 4.
5. Multiply line 27 of Form 1040 or Form 1040NR by line 4 5.
6. Subtract line 5 from line 2 6.
7. Enter the amount, if any, from line 28 of Form 1040 or Form 1040NR,
attributable to the same business for which the qualified health plan is
established 7.
8. Subtract line 7 from line 6 8.
9. Enter your Medicare wages (Form W-2, box 5) from an S corporation in
which you are a morethan-2% shareholder and in which the qualified health
plan is established 9.
10. Enter any amount from Form 2555, line 45, attributable to the amount
entered on line 2 or line 9 above, or any amount from Form 2555-EZ, line 18,
attributable to the amount entered on line 9 above 10.
Note. If you are not filing Form 2555 or 2555-EZ, enter -0-.

11. Subtract line 10 from line 8 or 9, whichever applies 11.
12. Enter your self-employed health insurance deduction for nonspecified
premiums from Worksheet P, line 3, or Worksheet 6-A, line 14, in chapter 6
of . 535. 12.

13. Subtract line 12 from line 11 13.
14. Enter the smaller of line 1 or line 13 14.
15. Add lines 12 and 14. Then use one of the methods that follow to figure
the PTC and the selfemployed health insurance deduction for specified
premiums 15.

*If you used either optional method to figure your net earnings from self-
employment from any business, do not enter your net profit from the
business. Instead, enter the amount attributable to that business from
Schedule SE, Section B, line 4b.

**Earned income includes net earnings and gains from the sale, transfer, or licensing of property you created. However, it does not include capital gain income.

Iterative Calculation Method

Follow the steps below to figure your self-employed health insurance deduction and PTC under the Iterative Calculation Method. You do not have to use this method. You can use the Simplified Calculation Method (discussed later) or any computation method that satisfies each set of rules as long as the sum of the deduction claimed for the premiums and the PTC computed, taking the deduction into account, is less than or equal to the premiums.

Do not round to whole dollars when performing the computations under this method. Instead, use dollars and cents. This is necessary so you can complete Step 6.

Step 1. Figure your adjusted gross income (AGI), modified AGI, and household income using Worksheet X, line 15, as your self-employed health insurance deduction. Use Worksheets 1-1 and 1-2 in the Form 8962 instructions to figure modified AGI and household income.

If you are claiming any of the following deductions or exclusions, see Special Instructions for SelfEmployed Individuals Who Claim Certain Deductions/Exclusions (discussed later) before you complete Step 1.

1. Passive activity losses from rental real estate activities and lines 1d and 4 of Form 8582 are losses.
2. IRA deduction.

3. Exclusion of interest from series EE and I U.S. savings bonds issued after 1989.
4. Student loan interest deduction.
5. Tuition and fees deduction.
6. Domestic production activities deduction.

Step 2. Figure the total PTC on Form 8962 using the AGI, modified AGI, and household income you determined in Step 1. Enter the modified AGI and household income from Step 1 on the Form 8962. When figuring the PTC, use all enrollment premiums for qualified health plans in which you or an individual in your tax family enrolled. Complete this Form 8962 only through line 24. Do not attach this Form 8962 to your tax return.

Note.

If you are not eligible to take the PTC, stop here. Do not use this method. Instead, figure your selfemployed health insurance deduction using the Self-Employed Health Insurance Deduction Worksheet in the Form 1040 or Form 1040NR instructions or, if required, Worksheet 6-A in chapter 6 of . 535. If you are following the instructions under Special Instructions for Self-Employed Individuals Who Claim Certain Deductions/Exclusions, make this determination when you complete the final iteration of Step 2.

Step 3. Figure your self-employed health insurance deduction for specified premiums by completing the following worksheet.
If you have more than one trade or business under which you established a qualified health plan, see More than one trade or business below before you complete the Step 3 Worksheet.
Step 3 Worksheet
Note. Enter amounts in dollars and cents. Do not round to whole dollars.
1. Enter the amount from Worksheet W, line 5. If you did not complete Worksheet W, enter the amount from Worksheet X, line 1
1. .

Caution:If the amounts on lines 12–23, column E, of your Step 2 Form 8962 are not the same for each month and you had specified premiums for fewer than 12 months, skip lines 2–5 below and enter on line 6 the total of those column E amounts for the months you paid specified premiums.

2. Enter the total PTC (Form 8962, line 24) you figured in Step 2, earlier
2. . 3. Enter the number of months in 2014 for which specified premiums were paid 3.
Note. Self-employment for part of a month counts as a full month of self-employment.
4. Enter the number of months someone in your coverage family was enrolled in the qualified health plan 4.
5. Divide line 3 by line 4 5.
6. Multiply line 5 by line 2 6. .
7. Subtract line 6 from line 1 7. .
8. Enter the amount from Worksheet X, line 14

8. .
9. Enter the smaller of line 7 or line 8. Then go to Step 4 next.
9. .

More than one trade or business. If you have more than one trade or business under which you established a qualified health plan, you must complete lines 1-7 separately for each trade or business. Use the following instructions to complete the Step 3 Worksheet.

Line 1. Enter the amounts for the separate trade or business.

If the Caution under line 1 applies to you, skip lines 2-5. Enter on line 6 the total of the column E amounts for the months you paid specified premiums that are allocable to the specified premiums you entered on line 1 for the separate trade or business. You can allocate the column E amounts using any reasonable method. One reasonable method is based on enrollment premiums for each plan. Under this method, multiply the total of the column E amounts for the months you paid specified premiums by a fraction. The numerator of the fraction is the amount of specified premiums you entered on line 1 for the separate trade or business. The denominator of the fraction is the total of the column A amounts for the months you paid specified premiums.

Line 2. Enter the Step 2 PTC that is allocable to the specified premiums you entered on line 1 for the separate trade or business. You can allocate the Step 2 PTC using any reasonable method. One reasonable method is based on enrollment premiums for each plan. Under this method, multiply the Step 2 PTC by a fraction. The numerator of the fraction is the amount of specified premiums you entered on line 1 for the separate trade or business. The denominator of the fraction is the amount on line 11, column A, or the total of lines 12-23, column A, of the Step 2 Form 8962.

Lines 3-6. Complete these lines for the plan established under the separate trade or business.
Line 7. After you complete this line for each trade or business, add the amounts on line 7 for all the trades or businesses. Use the total of the line 7 amounts to complete lines 8 and 9. Lines 8-9. Complete these lines once for all trades or businesses.

Step 4. Refigure the total PTC on another Form 8962. Complete this Form 8962 through line 29. When refiguring the total PTC, use all enrollment premiums for qualified health plans in which you or any individual in your tax family enrolled. Determine AGI, modified AGI, and household income using the total of the Step 3 Worksheet, line 9, and Worksheet X, line 12, as your self-employed health insurance deduction. Use Worksheets 1-1 and 1-2 in the Form 8962 instructions to figure modified AGI and household income.

Step 5. Refigure your self-employed health health deduction for specified premiums by completing the Step 5 Worksheet.
If you have more than one trade or business under which you established a qualified health plan, see More than one trade or business later before you complete the Step 5 Worksheet.
Step 5 Worksheet
Note. Enter amounts in dollars and cents. Do not round to whole dollars.
1. Enter the amount from line 1 of the Step 3 Worksheet
1. .

Caution:If you skipped lines 2–5 of the Step 3 Worksheet, skip lines 2 and 3 below and enter on line 4 the total of the column E amounts from your Step 4 Form 8962 for the months you paid specified premiums.

2. Enter the total PTC (Form 8962, line 24) you figured in Step 4, earlier
2. .
3. Enter the amount from line 5 of the Step 3 Worksheet
3.
4. Multiply line 3 by line 2 4. .
5. Subtract line 4 from line 1 5. .
6. Enter the amount from Worksheet X, line 14
6. .
7. Enter the smaller of line 5 or line 6. Then go to Step 6 next 7. .

More than one trade or business. If you have more than one trade or business under which you established a qualified health plan, you must complete lines 1-5 separately for each trade or business. Use the following instructions to complete the Step 5 Worksheet.

Line 1. Enter the amount from the Step 3 Worksheet for the same separate trade or business for which you are completing the Step 5 Worksheet.

If the Caution under line 1 applies to you, skip lines 2 and 3. Enter on line 4 the total of the column E amounts for the months you paid specified premiums that are allocable to the specified premiums you entered on line 1 for the separate trade or business. Allocate the column E amounts using the same method you used on the Step 3 Worksheet.

Line 2. Enter the Step 4 PTC that is allocable to the premiums you entered on line 1 for the separate trade or business. Use the same allocation method you used on the Step 3 Worksheet.
Line 3. Enter the amount from the Step 3 Worksheet for the same separate trade or business for which you are completing the Step 5 Worksheet.
Line 5. After you complete this line for each trade or business, add the amounts on line 5 for all the trades or businesses. Use the total of the line 5 amounts to complete lines 6 and 7.
Lines 6-7. Complete these lines once for all trades or businesses.
Step 6. Answer the following 3 questions.
1. Is the change in the self-employed health insurance deduction from Step 3 to Step 5 less than $1.00?
❏ Yes❏ No
2. Is the change in the total PTC from Step 2 to Step 4 less than $1.00?
❏ Yes❏ No
3. Did you answer "Yes" to both questions 1 and 2?

❏ Yes. You can claim a PTC for the amount you figured in Step 4. Attach the Form 8962 you used in Step 4 to your tax return. You can claim a self-employed health insurance deduction for the specified premiums equal to the amount on line 7 of the Step 5 Worksheet.

Note. Your self-employed health insurance deduction is the total of the Step 5 Worksheet, line 7, and Worksheet X, line 12. Enter this total on line 29 of Form 1040 or 1040NR.
❏ No. Repeat Step 4 and Step 5 (using amounts determined in the immediately preceding step) until changes in both the self-employed health insurance deduction and the total PTC between steps are less than $1.00.

If you are unable to complete Step 6 because changes between steps are always $1.00 or more, do not use the Iterative Calculation Method. Instead, use the Simplified Calculation Method or any computation method that satisfies the rules for the self-employed health insurance deduction and PTC as long as the sum of the deduction claimed for the premiums and the PTC computed, taking the deduction into account, is less than or equal to the premiums.

Simplified Calculation Method

Follow the steps below to figure your self-employed health insurance deduction and PTC under the Simplified Calculation Method. You do not have to use this method. You can use the Iterative Calculation Method (discussed earlier) if you can complete Step 6 of that method or you can use any computation method that satisfies each set of rules as long as the sum of the deduction claimed for the premiums and the PTC computed, taking the deduction into account, is less than or equal to the premiums.

Step 1. Figure your adjusted gross income (AGI), modified AGI, and household income using the total of Worksheet X, line 15, as your self-employed health insurance deduction. Use Worksheets 1-1 and 1-2 in the Form 8962 instructions to figure modified AGI and household income.

If you are claiming any of the following deductions or exclusions, see Special Instructions for SelfEmployed Individuals Who Claim Certain Deductions/Exclusions (discussed later) before you complete Step 1.

1. Passive activity losses from rental real estate activities and lines 1d and 4 of Form 8582 are losses.
2. IRA deduction.
3. Exclusion of interest from series EE and I U.S. savings bonds issued after 1989.
4. Student loan interest deduction.
5. Tuition and fees deduction.
6. Domestic production activities deduction.

Step 2. Figure the total PTC on Form 8962 using the AGI, modified AGI, and household income you determined in Step 1. Enter the modified AGI and household income from Step 1 on the Form 8962. When figuring the PTC, use all enrollment premiums for qualified health plans in which you or any individual in your tax family enrolled. Complete this Form 8962 only through line 24. Do not attach this Form 8962 to your tax return.

Note.

If you are not eligible to take the PTC, stop here. Do not use this method. Instead, figure your selfemployed health insurance deduction using the Self-

Employed Health Insurance Deduction Worksheet in the Form 1040 or Form 1040NR instructions or, if required, Worksheet 6-A in chapter 6 of . 535. If you are following the instructions under Special Instructions for Self-Employed Individuals Who Claim Certain Deductions/Exclusions, make this determination when you complete the final iteration of Step 2.

Step 3. Figure your self-employed health insurance deduction by completing the following worksheet.
If you have more than one trade or business under which you established a qualified health plan, see More than one trade or business below before you complete the Step 3 Worksheet.
Step 3 Worksheet
1. Enter the amount from Worksheet W, line 5. If you did not complete Worksheet W, enter the amount from Worksheet X, line 1
1.

Caution:If the amounts on lines 12–23, column E, of your Step 2 Form 8962 are not the same for each month and you had specified premiums for fewer than 12 months, skip lines 2–5 below and enter on line 6 the total of those column E amounts for the months you paid specified premiums.

2. Enter the total PTC (Form 8962, line 24) you figured in Step 2, earlier
2.
3. Enter the number of months in 2014 for which specified premiums were paid 3.
Note. Self-employment for part of a month counts as a full month of self-employment.
4. Enter the number of months someone in your coverage family was enrolled in the qualified health plan 4.
5. Divide line 3 by line 4 5.
6. Multiply line 5 by line 2 6.
7. Subtract line 6 from line 1 7. 8. Enter the amount from Worksheet X, line 14
8.
9. Enter the smaller of line 7 or line 8 9.
10. Enter the amount from Worksheet X, line 12
10.
11. Add lines 9 and 10. Use this amount as your self-employed health insurance deduction in Step 4 next. Also enter this amount on line 29 of Form

1040 or Form 1040NR 11.

More than one trade or business. If you have more than one trade or business under which you established a qualified health plan, you must complete lines 1-7 separately for each trade or business. Use the following instructions to complete the Step 3 Worksheet.

Line 1. Enter the amounts for the separate trade or business.

If the Caution under line 1 applies to you, skip lines 2-5. Enter on line 6 the total of the column E amounts for the months you paid specified premiums that are allocable to the specified premiums you entered on line 1 for the separate trade or business. You can allocate the column E amounts using any reasonable method. One reasonable method is based on enrollment premiums for each plan. Under this method, multiply the total of the column E amounts for the months you paid specified premiums by a fraction. The numerator of the fraction is the amount of specified premiums you entered on line 1 for the separate trade or business. The denominator of the fraction is the total of the column A amounts for the months you paid specified premiums.

Line 2. Enter the Step 2 PTC that is allocable to the specified premiums you entered on line 1 for the separate trade or business. You can allocate the Step 2 PTC using any reasonable method. One reasonable method is based on enrollment premiums for each plan. Under this method, multiply the Step 2 PTC by a fraction. The numerator of the fraction is the amount of specified premiums you entered on line 1 for the separate trade or business. The denominator of the fraction is the amount on line 11, column A, or the total of lines 12-23, column A, of the Step 2 Form 8962.

Lines 3-6. Complete these lines for the plan established under the separate trade or business.
Line 7. After you complete this line for each trade or business, add the amounts on line 7 for all the trades or businesses. Use the total of the line 7 amounts to complete lines 8-11.
Line 8-11. Complete these lines once for all trades or businesses.

Step 4. Refigure the final PTC on another Form 8962. Complete this Form 8962 through line 29. Attach this Form 8962 to your tax return. When refiguring the PTC, use all enrollment premiums for qualified health plans in which you or any individual in your tax family enrolled. Determine AGI, modified AGI, and household income using the amount from line 11 of the Step 3 Worksheet as your self-employed health insurance deduction. Use Worksheets 1-1 and 1-2 in the Form 8962 instructions to figure modified AGI and household income.

Special Instructions for Self-Employed Individuals Who Claim Certain Deductions/Exclusions
The instructions in this section apply to you if you claim any of the following deductions or exclusions.
1. Passive activity losses from rental real estate activities and lines 1d and 4 of Form 8582 are losses.
2. IRA deduction.
3. Exclusion of interest from series EE and I U.S. savings bonds issued after 1989.
4. Student loan interest deduction.
5. Tuition and fees deduction.
6. Domestic production activities deduction.

Read the following instructions if you are claiming one or more of the deductions/exclusions listed above. Read these instructions before you complete the Iterative Calculation Method or Simplified Calculation Method.

1. The first time you complete the Iterative Calculation Method or Simplified Calculation Method, you do so without including any of the deductions/exclusions listed above in AGI, modified AGI, or household income. If you use the Simplified Calculation Method, complete it only through Step 3. Enter "400" on Form 8962, line 5, if the result of dividing line 3 by line 4 is more than 400.

2. After you complete (1), figure the deduction/exclusion using the appropriate form or worksheet in your tax return instructions. When figuring modified AGI on the form or worksheet (or AGI on Form 8903), use as your self-employed health insurance deduction the amount from Step 6 of the Iterative Calculation Method or Step 3 of the Simplified Calculation Method.

If you are claiming more than 1 deduction/exclusion on the list, you must figure the deductions/exclusions in the order shown in the list. For example, if you are claiming the student loan interest deduction and the exclusion of interest from series EE and I U.S. savings bonds, you must figure the exclusion of interest from series EE and I U.S. savings bonds first and complete (3) and (4) or (5) using that deduction. Then you figure the student loan interest deduction, as explained in (5) or at the end of Worksheets Y and Z.

3. Enter the deduction/exclusion you figured in (2) on your tax return.

4. If you completed Worksheet W, complete Worksheet Y and follow the instructions under line 18 of that Worksheet. Skip (5).
5. If you did not complete Worksheet W, do the following.

a. Repeat the Iterative Calculation Method or Simplified Calculation Method. Use the amount from (2) in any step that requires you to figure AGI, modified AGI, and household income.

b. If the amount from (2) is the only deduction/exclusion on the list you are claiming, complete either method through the last step and follow the step instructions for claiming the PTC and selfemployed health insurance deduction on your return. Skip (c).

c. If the amount from (2) is not the only deduction/exclusion on the list you are claiming, complete the Iterative Calculation Method through Step 6 or the Simplified Calculation Method through Step 3. Then figure the additional deduction/exclusion using the appropriate form or worksheet in your tax return instructions. When figuring modified AGI on the form or worksheet (or AGI on Form 8903), use as your self-employed health insurance deduction the amount from Step 6 of the Iterative Calculation Method or Step 3 of the Simplified Calculation Method. Then repeat (3) and (5) for each additional deduction/exclusion. Follow (5b) for your final deduction/exclusion.

Worksheet Y. Refiguring Household Income, the Limitation on Additional Tax, and the Limit Under Section 5.03 of Revenue Procedure 2014-41
1. Enter the amount from Worksheet W, line 15
1.
2. Enter the deduction or exclusion 2.
3. Revised household income. Subtract line 2 from line 1 3.
4. Enter $600 ($300 if your filing status is single) 4.
5. 5. 5.

6. Enter the amount from Worksheet W, line 18b
6.

7. Divide line 5 by line 6. Enter the result rounded to a whole percentage. For example, enter 154 if the percentage is 1.542 and enter 155 if the percentage is 1.549. See Lines 19, 22, and 25 under Instructions for Worksheet W, earlier, for special rules

7.
• If the result is less than 200, enter the amount from line 4 on line 14. Skip lines 8-13.
• If the result is 200 or more, go to line 8.
8. Enter $1,500 ($750 if your filing status is single) 8. 9. 9. 9.

10. Divide line 9 by line 6. Enter the result rounded to a whole percentage. For example, enter 154 if the percentage is 1.542 and enter 155 if the percentage is 1.549. See Lines 19, 22, and 25 under Instructions for Worksheet W, earlier, for special rules

• If the result is less than 300, enter the amount from line 8 on line 14. Skip lines 11-13.
• If the result is 300 or more, go to line 11. 10.
11. Enter $2,500 ($1,250 if your filing status is single) 11.
12. Subtract line 11 from line 3. If zero or less, enter -0-. 12.

13. Divide line 12 by line 6. Enter the result rounded to a whole percentage. For example, enter 154 if the percentage is 1.542 and enter 155 if the percentage is 1.549. See Lines 19, 22, and 25 under Instructions for Worksheet W, earlier, for special rules.

• If the result is less than 400, enter the amount from line 11 on line 14.
• If the result is 400 or more, enter the amount from Worksheet W, line 6, on line 14.
13.
14. Enter the amount you were instructed to enter here by line 7, 10, or 13.
14.
15. Enter the amount from Worksheet W, line 7
15.
16. Add lines 14 and 15. 16.
17. Enter the smaller of line 16 above or line 5 of Worksheet W.

17.

18. Is line 17 above equal to line 28 of Worksheet W?

❑ Yes. Skip lines 19-21. Enter the amount from Worksheet X, line 15, on line 22 below. Then see Next under line 22 for further instructions.

❑ No. Go to line 19. 18.

19. Enter the amount from Worksheet X, line 12 20. Enter the amount from Worksheet X, line 13

20.

21. Enter the smaller of line 17 or line 20 21.

22. Add lines 19 and 21. Then see Next below for further instructions 22.

Next. Repeat the Iterative Calculation Method or Simplified Calculation Method, whichever applies. In Step 1 of either method, use the amount on line 22 above as your self-employed health insurance deduction. Also use the amount on line 2 above in any step that requires you to figure AGI, modified AGI, and household income. If the amount on line 2 above is the only deduction/exclusion on the list that you are claiming, complete either method through the last step. If you are claiming another deduction/exclusion on the list, do the following.

• When you repeat either method as explained above, complete the Iterative Calculation Method through Step 6 or complete the Simplified Calculation Method through Step 3.

• Figure the other deduction/exclusion using the appropriate form or the worksheet provided in your tax return instructions. Use the self-employed health insurance deduction you figured in either Step 6 of the Iterative Calculation Method or Step 3 of the Simplified Calculation Method to figure modified AGI for the other deduction/exclusion (or AGI for the domestic production activities deduction).

• Then complete Worksheet Z, later, for the other deduction/exclusion. Worksheet Z. Refiguring Household Income, the Limitation on Additional Tax, and the Limit Under Section 5.03 of Revenue Procedure 2014-41

Note. Complete Worksheet Y before you complete Worksheet Z.

1. Enter the amount from Worksheet Y, line 3

1.

2. Enter the deduction or exclusion 2.

3. Revised household income. Subtract line 2 from line 1 3.

4. Enter $600 ($300 if your filing status is single) 4.
5. 5. 5.

6. Enter the amount from Worksheet W, line 18b
7. Divide line 5 by line 6. Enter the result rounded to a whole percentage. For example, enter 154 if the percentage is 1.542 and enter 155 if the percentage is 1.549. See Lines 19, 22, and 25 under Instructions for Worksheet W, earlier, for special rules

7.
• If the result is less than 200, enter the amount from line 4 on line 14. Skip lines 8-13.
• If the result is 200 or more, go to line 8.
8. Enter $1,500 ($750 if your filing status is single) 8.
9. 9. 9.

10. Divide line 9 by line 6. Enter the result rounded to a whole percentage. For example, enter 154 if the percentage is 1.542 and enter 155 if the percentage is 1.549. See Lines 19, 22, and 25 under Instructions for Worksheet W, earlier, for special rules

10.
• If the result is less than 300, enter the amount from line 8 on line 14. Skip lines 11-13.
• If the result is 300 or more, go to line 11.
11. Enter $2,500 ($1,250 if your filing status is single) 11.
12. Subtract line 11 from line 3. If zero or less, enter -0-. 12.

13. Divide line 12 by line 6. Enter the result rounded to a whole percentage. For example, enter 154 if the percentage is 1.542 and enter 155 if the percentage is 1.549. See Lines 19, 22, and 25 under Instructions for Worksheet W, earlier, for special rules.

• If the result is less than 400, enter the amount from line 11 on line 14.
• If the result is 400 or more, enter the amount from Worksheet W, line 6, on line 14.
13.
14. Enter the amount you were instructed to enter here by line 7, 10, or 13.
14.
15. Enter the amount from Worksheet W, line 7

15.

16. Add lines 14 and 15. 16.

17. Enter the smaller of line 16 above or line 5 of Worksheet W. 18. Is line 17 above equal to line 17 of Worksheet Y?

❏ Yes. Skip lines 19-21. Enter the amount from Worksheet Y, line 22, on line 22 below. Then see Next under line 22 for further instructions.

❏ No. Go to line 19. 18.

19. Enter the amount from Worksheet X, line 12

19.

20. Enter the amount from Worksheet X, line 13

20.

21. Enter the smaller of line 17 or line 20 21.

22. Add lines 19 and 21. Then see Next below for further instructions 22.

Next. Repeat the Iterative Calculation Method or Simplified Calculation Method, whichever applies. In Step 1 of either method, use the amount on line 22 above as your self-employed health insurance deduction. Also use the amounts on line 2 of Worksheets Y and Z in any step that requires you to figure AGI, modified AGI, and household income. If you are not claiming any more deductions/exclusions on the list, complete either method through the last step and follow the step instructions for claiming the PTC and self-employed health insurance deduction on your tax return. If you are claiming another deduction/exclusion on the list, do the following.

• When you repeat either method as explained above, complete the Iterative Calculation Method through Step 6 or complete the Simplified Calculation Method through Step 3.

• Figure the other deduction/exclusion using the appropriate form or the worksheet provided in your tax return instructions. Use the self-employed health insurance deduction you figured in either Step 6 of the Iterative Calculation Method or Step 3 of the Simplified Calculation Method to figure modified AGI for the other deduction/exclusion (or AGI for the domestic production activities deduction).

• Then complete another Worksheet Z for the other deduction/exclusion.
Illustrated Example of the Simplified Calculation Method
The following example illustrates the Simplified Calculation Method.

In 2014, Carla Birch, her husband Jim, and their 2 dependent children enrolled in the applicable SLCSP through the Marketplace. The annual premium was $12,000, and $4,200 in APTC was paid for Carla, her husband and 2 dependent children. All of the premiums are specified premiums. Carla operated a business as a sole proprietorship during the entire year. Carla and Jim are filing a joint Form 1040 (not illustrated). The income and deductions on page 1 of their Form 1040 (excluding line 29) consist of the following.

Jim's salary (Form 1040, line 7) $56,625
Taxable interest (Form 1040, line 8a) 419
Carla's net profit from her business on Schedule C (Form 1040, line 12) 30,000
Total income (Form 1040, line 22) 87,044
Deductible part of Carla's self-employment tax (Form 1040, line 27) 2,119
Carla's qualified retirement plan deduction (Form 1040, line 28) 2,500
Carla's Worksheet W

Because Carla had APTC during the months of self-employment, she begins by completing Worksheet W, Parts I and III, as shown later. She skips Part II because neither one of her children is required to file a Federal income tax return for 2014.

Line 1. Carla enters $87,044, which is the total income shown on line 22 of her Form 1040. Total income is the sum of Jim's salary, taxable interest, and Carla's net profit.
Line 4a. Carla enters $4,619. This is the total of the deductible part of her self-employment tax and her qualified retirement plan deduction.
Line 18b. Carla enters $23,550. This is the Federal poverty line shown in Table 1-1 in the Form 8962 instructions for a family size of 4.
Carla's Worksheet X

After completing Worksheet W, Carla completes Worksheet X to determine how much of the $10,300 on Worksheet W, line 28, can be used in figuring the first iteration of the PTC under the Simplified Calculation Method. She can use the full $10,300 as shown on Worksheet X, line 14.

Carla's Worksheet W. Figuring Household Income and the Limitation on Additional Tax
Part I: Taxpayer's Modified AGI

1. Combine the amounts from:
• Form 1040, lines 8b, 22, and the excess, if any, of line 20a over line 20b.
• Form 1040NR, lines 9b and 23 1. 87,044
Note. See instructions if you are filing Form 8582, 8814, or 8815.
2. Enter any amounts from Form 2555, lines 45 and 50, and Form 2555-EZ, line 18 2. 3. Add lines 1 and 2 3. 87,044
4a. Enter the total of the amounts from:
• Form 1040, lines 23 through 28, 30, and 31a, plus any write-in adjustments you entered on the dotted line next to line 36.
• Form 1040NR, lines 24 through 28, 30, and 31, plus any write-in adjustments you entered on the dotted line next to line 35 4a. 4,619
4b. Enter your self-employed health insurance deduction for nonspecified premiums from Worksheet P, line 3, or Worksheet 6-A, line 14, in chapter 6 of . 535 4b.
5. Enter specified premiums (see Specified premiums under Instructions for Worksheet P, earlier)
5. 12,000
6. Enter APTC attributable to the premiums on line 5 (see instructions) 6. 4,200
7. Subtract line 6 from line 5 7. 7,800
8. Add lines 4a, 4b, and 7 8. 12,419
9. Subtract line 8 from line 3. Then go to Part II if you are claiming dependents on your tax return. If you are not claiming any dependents on your tax return, skip Part II and go to Part III 9. 74,625
Part II: Dependents' Modified AGI
Note. Lines 10–14 of this part are omitted because Carla's dependent children are not required to file Federal tax returns.
Part III: Limitation on Additional Tax
15. Household income. Add lines 9 and 14 15. 74,625
16. Enter $600 ($300 if your filing status is single) 16. 600
17. 17. 17. 74,025
18a. Enter the number of exemptions from Form 1040, line 6d, or Form 1040NR, line 7d 18a. 4
18b. Enter the Federal poverty amount as determined by the family size on line 18a and Federal poverty Table 1-1, 1-2, or 1-3 for your state of residence during 2014 in the Form 8962 instructions

18b. 23,550

19. Divide line 17 by line 18b. Enter the result rounded to a whole percentage. For example, enter 154 if the percentage is 1.542 and enter 155 if the percentage is 1.549. See the instructions for lines 19, 22, and 25 for special rules 19. 314

• If the result is less than 200, enter the amount from line 16 on line 26. Skip lines 20–25.
• If the result is 200 or more, go to line 20.
20. Enter $1,500 ($750 if your filing status is single) 20. 1,500
21. 21. 21. 73,125

22. Divide line 21 by line 18b. Enter the result rounded to a whole percentage. For example, enter
154 if the percentage is 1.542 and enter 155 if the percentage is 1.549. See the instructions for lines 19,
22, and 25 for special rules 22. 311

• If the result is less than 300, enter the amount from line 20 on line 26. Skip lines 23–25.
• If the result is 300 or more, go to line 23.
23. Enter $2,500 ($1,250 if your filing status is single) 23. 2,500
24. 24. 24. 72,125

25. Divide line 24 by line 18b. Enter the result rounded to a whole percentage. For example, enter
154 if the percentage is 1.542 and enter 155 if the percentage is 1.549. See the instructions for lines 19,
22, and 25 for special rules 25. 306

• If the result is less than 400, enter the amount from line 23 on line 26.
• If the result is 400 or more, enter the amount from line 6 on line 26.
26. Enter the amount you were instructed to enter here by line 19, 22, or 2526. 2,500
27. Add lines 7 and 26. 27. 10,300
28. Enter the smaller of line 5 or line 27. Then go to Worksheet X
28. 10,300
Carla's Worksheet X. Figuring the Limit Under Section 5.03 of Revenue Procedure 2014-41
1. Enter the amount from Worksheet W, line 28. If you did not complete

Worksheet W, enter your specified premiums. See Specified premiums under Instructions for Worksheet P, earlier

1. 10,300
2. Enter your net profit* and any other earned income** from the business under which the qualified health plan is established. Do not include Conservation Reserve Program payments exempt from self-employment tax. If the business is an S corporation, skip to line 9 2. 30,000

3. Enter the total of all net profits* from: Schedule C (Form 1040), line 31; Schedule C-EZ (Form
1040), line 3; Schedule F (Form 1040), line 34; or Schedule K-1 (Form 1065), box 14, code A; plus any other income allocable to the profitable businesses. Do not include Conservation Reserve Program payments exempt from self-employment tax. See the Instructions for Schedule SE (Form 1040). Do not include any net losses shown on these schedules 3. 30,000

4. Divide line 2 by line 3 4. 1.0
5. Multiply line 27 of Form 1040 or Form 1040NR by line 4 5. 2,119
6. Subtract line 5 from line 2 6. 27,881
7. Enter the amount, if any, from line 28 of Form 1040 or Form 1040NR, attributable to the same business for which the qualified health plan is established 7. 2,500
8. Subtract line 7 from line 6 8. 25,381
9. Enter your Medicare wages (Form W-2, box 5) from an S corporation in which you are a morethan-2% shareholder and in which the qualified health plan is established 9.
10. Enter any amount from Form 2555, line 45, attributable to the amount entered on line 2 or line 9 above, or any amount from Form 2555-EZ, line 18, attributable to the amount entered on line 9 above 10. 0
Note. If you are not filing Form 2555 or 2555-EZ, enter -0-.
11. Subtract line 10 from line 8 or 9, whichever applies 11. 25,381
12. Enter your self-employed health insurance deduction for nonspecified premiums from Worksheet P, line 3, or Worksheet 6-A, line 14, in chapter 6 of . 535 12.
13. Subtract line 12 from line 11 13. 25,381
14. Enter the smaller of line 1 or line 13 14. 10,300
15. Add lines 12 and 14. Then use one of the methods that follow to figure the PTC and the selfemployed health insurance deduction for specified

premiums 15. 10,300

*If you used either optional method to figure your net earnings from self-employment, do not enter your net profit. Instead, enter the amount from Schedule SE, Section B, line 4b.

**Earned income includes net earnings and gains from the sale, transfer, or licensing of property you created. However, it does not include capital gain income. If you were a more-than-2% shareholder in the S corporation under which the insurance plan is established, earned income is your Medicare wages (box 5 of Form W-2) from that corporation.

The Simplified Calculation Method for Carla

Step 1. Carla figures her AGI, modified AGI, and household income using $10,300 as the self-employed health insurance deduction. (She does not enter $10,300 on Form 1040, line 29.) Her AGI is $72,125, figured as follows.

Total income from Form 1040, line 22 $87,044
Minus: deductible part of self-employment tax (2,119)
Minus: qualified retirement plan deduction (2,500)
Minus: self-employed health insurance deduction from Worksheet X, line 15 (10,300)
Equals: AGI 72,125

Carla uses this AGI amount on Worksheet 1-1. Taxpayer's Modified AGI Worksheet—Line 2a (not illustrated) in the Form 8962 instructions to figure her modified AGI and household income. Her modified AGI and household income are each $72,125, the same as her AGI figured in this Step 1.

Step 2. Carla figures the total PTC on Form 8962 using the modified AGI and household income figured in Step 1. This Form 8962 is shown later in this . for purposes of illustration and labeled "Carla's Step 2 PTC." She completes this Form 8962 only through line 24. She uses the total PTC shown on line 24 ($5,148) to figure the self-employed health insurance deduction in Step 3, later. She does not attach this Form 8962 to her tax return.

Step 3. Carla completes the following worksheet to figure the self-employed health insurance deduction she will enter on Form 1040, line 29.
Carla's Step 3 Worksheet
1. Enter the amount from Worksheet W, line 5. If you did not complete

Worksheet W, enter the amount from Worksheet X, line 1
1. 12,000

Caution:If the amounts on lines 12–23, column E, of your Step 2 Form 8962 are not the same for each month and you had specified premiums for fewer than 12 months, skip lines 2–5 below and enter on line 6 the total of those column E amounts for the months you paid specified premiums. 2. Enter the total PTC (Form 8962, line 24) you figured in Step 2, earlier

2. 5,148
3. Enter the number of months in 2014 for which specified premiums were paid 3. 12
Note. Self-employment for part of a month counts as a full month of self-employment.
4. Enter the number of months someone in your coverage family was enrolled in the qualified health plan 4. 12
5. Divide line 3 by line 4 5. 1.0
6. Multiply line 5 by line 2 6. 5,148
7. Subtract line 6 from line 1 7. 6,852
8. Enter the amount from Worksheet X, line 14
8. 10,300
9. Enter the smaller of line 7 or line 8 9. 6,852
10. Enter the amount from Worksheet X, line 12
10. 0
11. Add lines 9 and 10. Use this amount as your self-employed health insurance deduction in Step 4 next. Also enter this amount on line 29 of Form 1040 or Form 1040NR 11. 6,852

Step 4. Carla refigures the final PTC on another Form 8962. This Form 8962 is shown later in this . for purposes of illustration and is labeled "Carla's Step 4 PTC." Carla figures AGI, modified AGI, and household income using the amount from line 11 of the Step 3 Worksheet as her self-employed health insurance deduction. Her AGI is $75,573, figured as follows.

Total income from Form 1040, line 22 $87,044
Minus: deductible part of self-employment tax (2,119)
Minus: qualified retirement plan deduction (2,500)
Minus: self-employed health insurance deduction from line 11 of the Step 3 Worksheet (6,852)

Equals: AGI 75,573

Carla uses this AGI amount on Worksheet 1-1. Taxpayer's Modified AGI Worksheet—Line 2a (not illustrated) in the Form 8962 instructions to refigure her modified AGI and household income. Her modified AGI and household income are each $75,573, the same as her AGI figured above.

Carla completes Form 8962 through line 26. She enters the amount from line 26 ($621) on Form 1040, line 69, and attaches Form 8962.
This image is too large to be displayed in the current screen. Please click the link to view the image.
Carla's Step 2 PTC
This image is too large to be displayed in the current screen. Please click the link to view the image.
Carla's Step 4 PTC
How To Get Tax Help
Do you need help with a tax issue or preparing your tax return, or do you need a free . or form?
Preparing and filing your tax return. Find free options to prepare and file your return on IRS.gov or in your local community if you qualify.
• Go to IRS.gov and click on the Filing tab to see your options.
• Enter "Free File" in the search box to use brand name software to prepare and e-file your federal tax return for free.

• Enter "VITA" in the search box, download the free IRS2Go app, or call 1-800-906-9887 to find the nearest Volunteer Income Tax Assistance or Tax Counseling for the Elderly (TCE) location for free tax preparation.

• Enter "TCE" in the search box, download the free IRS2Go app, or call 1-888-227-7669 to find the nearest Tax Counseling for the Elderly location for free tax preparation.

The Volunteer Income Tax Assistance (VITA) program offers free tax help to people who generally make $53,000 or less, persons with disabilities, the elderly, and limited-English-speaking taxpayers who need help preparing their own tax returns. The Tax Counseling for the Elderly (TCE) program offers free tax help for all taxpayers, particularly those who are 60 years of age and older. TCE volunteers specialize in answering questions about pensions and retirement-related issues unique to seniors.

Getting answers to your tax law questions. IRS.gov and IRS2Go are ready when you are—24 hours a day, 7 days a week.

• Enter "ITA" in the search box on IRS.gov for the Interactive Tax Assistant, a tool that will ask you questions on a number of tax law topics and provide answers. You can print the entire interview and the final response.

• Enter "Tax Map" or "Tax Trails" in the search box for detailed information by tax topic.
• Enter "Pub 17" in the search box to get Pub. 17, Your Federal Income Tax for Individuals, which features details on tax-saving opportunities, 2014 tax changes, and thousands of interactive links to help you find answers to your questions.

• Call TeleTax at 1-800-829-4477 for recorded information on a variety of tax topics.
• Access tax law information in your electronic filing software.
• Go to IRS.gov and click on the Help & Resources tab for more information. Tax forms and .s. You can download or print all of the forms and .s you may need on www.irs.gov/formspubs. Otherwise, you can:
• Go to www.irs.gov/orderforms to place an order and have forms mailed to you, or
• Call 1-800-829-3676 to order current-year forms, instructions, .s, and prior-year forms and instructions (limited to 5 years).
You should receive your order within 10 business days.
Where to file your tax return.
• There are many ways to file your return electronically. It's safe, quick and easy. See Preparing and filing your tax return, earlier, for more information.
• See your tax return instructions to determine where to mail your completed paper tax return.
Getting a transcript or copy of a return.
• Go to IRS.gov and click on "Get Transcript of Your Tax Records" under "Tools."
• Download the free IRS2Go app to your smart phone and use it to order transcripts of your tax returns or tax account.
• Call the transcript toll-free line at 1-800-908-9946.
• Mail Form 4506-T or Form 4506T-EZ (both available on IRS.gov).
Using online tools to help prepare your return. Go to IRS.gov and click on the Tools bar to use these and other self-service options.

• The Earned Income Tax Credit Assistant determines if you are eligible for the EIC.

• The First Time Homebuyer Credit Account Look-up tool provides information on your repayments and account balance.

• The Alternative Minimum Tax (AMT) Assistant determines whether you may be subject to AMT.

• The Online EIN Application helps you get an Employer Identification Number.

• The IRS Withholding Calculator estimates the amount you should have withheld from your paycheck for federal income tax purposes.

• The Electronic Filing PIN Request helps to verify your identity when you do not have your prior year AGI or prior year self-selected PIN available. Understanding identity theft issues.

• Go to www.irs.gov/uac/Identity-Protection for information and videos.

• If your SSN has been lost or stolen or you suspect you are a victim of tax-related identity theft, visit www.irs.gov/identitytheft to learn what steps you should take.

Checking on the status of a refund.

• Go to www.irs.gov/refunds.

• Download the free IRS2Go app to your smart phone and use it to check your refund status.

• Call the automated refund hotline at 1-800-829-1954.

Making a tax payment. You can make electronic payments online, by phone, or from a mobile device. Paying electronically is safe and secure. The IRS uses the latest encryption technology and does not store banking information. It's easy and secure and much quicker than mailing in a check or money order. Go to IRS.gov and click on the Payments tab or the "Pay Your Tax Bill" icon to make a payment using the following options.

• Direct Pay (only if you are an individual who has a checking or savings account).

• Debit or credit card.

• Electronic Federal Tax Payment System.

• Check or money order.

What if I can't pay now? Click on the Payments tab or the "Pay Your Tax Bill" icon on IRS.gov to find more information about these additional options.

• An online payment agreement determines if you are eligible to apply for an installment agreement if you cannot pay your taxes in full today. With the needed information, you can complete the application in about 30 minutes, and get immediate approval.

• An offer in compromise allows you to settle your tax debt for less than the full amount you owe. Use the Offer in Compromise Pre-Qualifier to confirm your eligibility.

Checking the status of an amended return. Go to IRS.gov and click on the Tools tab and then Where's My Amended Return?
Understanding an IRS notice or letter. Enter "Understanding your notice" in the search box on IRS.gov to find additional information about your IRS notice or letter.

Visiting the IRS. Locate the nearest Taxpayer Assistance Center using the Office Locator tool on IRS.gov. Enter "office locator" in the search box. Or choose the "Contact Us" option on the IRS2Go app and search Local Offices. Before you visit, use the Locator tool to check hours and services available.

Watching IRS videos. The IRS Video portal www.irsvideos.gov contains video and audio presentations on topics of interest to individuals, small businesses, and tax professionals. You'll find video clips of tax topics, archived versions of live panel discussions and Webinars, and audio archives of tax practitioner phone forums.

Getting tax information in other languages. For taxpayers whose native language is not English, we have the following resources available.
1. Taxpayers can find information on IRS.gov in the following languages.
a. Spanish.
b. Chinese.
c. Vietnamese.
d. Korean.
e. Russian.
2. The IRS Taxpayer Assistance Centers provide over-the-phone interpreter service in over 170 languages, and the service is available free to taxpayers.
The Taxpayer Advocate Service Is Here To Help You
What is the Taxpayer Advocate Service?

The Taxpayer Advocate Service (TAS) is an independent organization within the Internal Revenue Service that helps taxpayers and protects taxpayer rights. Our job is to ensure that every taxpayer is treated fairly and that you know and understand your rights under the Taxpayer Bill of Rights.

What Can the Taxpayer Advocate Service Do For You?

We can help you resolve problems that you can't resolve with the IRS. And our service is free. If you qualify for our assistance, you will be assigned to one advocate who will work with you throughout the process and will do everything possible to resolve your issue. TAS can help you if:

• Your problem is causing financial difficulty for you, your family, or your business,

• You face (or your business is facing) an immediate threat of adverse action, or
• You've tried repeatedly to contact the IRS but no one has responded, or the IRS hasn't responded by the date promised.

How Can You Reach Us?
We have offices in every state, the District of Columbia, and Puerto Rico. Your local advocate's number is in your local directory and at www.taxpayeradvocate.irs.gov. You can also call us at 1-877-777-4778.
How Can You Learn About Your Taxpayer Rights?

The Taxpayer Bill of Rights describes ten basic rights that all taxpayers have when dealing with the IRS. Our Tax Toolkit at www.taxpayeradvocate.irs.gov can help you understand what these rights mean to you and how they apply. These are your rights. Know them. Use them.

How Else Does the Taxpayer Advocate Service Help Taxpayers?
TAS works to resolve large-scale problems that affect many taxpayers. If you know of one of these broad issues, please report it to us at www.irs.gov/sams.
Low Income Taxpayer Clinics

Low Income Taxpayer Clinics (LITCs) serve individuals whose income is below a certain level and need to resolve tax problems such as audits, appeals, and tax collection disputes. Some clinics can provide information about taxpayer rights and responsibilities in different languages for individuals who speak English as a second language. To find a clinic near you, visit www.irs.gov/litc or see IRS . 4134, Low Income Taxpayer Clinic List.